Copyright © 2016 by Corso

All rights reserved.

No part of this book may be reproduced in any written, electronic, recording, or photocopying without written permission of the publisher or author. The exception would be in the case of brief quotations embodied in the critical articles or reviews and pages where permission is specifically granted by the publisher or author.

Although every precaution has been taken to verify the accuracy of the information contained herein, the author and publisher assume no responsibility for any errors or omissions. No liability is assumed for damages that may result from the use of information contained within.

Corso

Visit our website at www.corsosoftware.com

Report an error to info@corso3.com

Version 3.0

First Published: September 2015

CONTENTS

AGILE EA AND INNOVATION MANAGEMENT OVERVIEW	**11**
The importance of an agile approach to Enterprise Architecture	11
Linking innovation management and enterprise architecture	12
MANAGING CHANGE IN A TECHNOLOGICAL WORLD	**13**
Overview	13
Collecting & Harvesting New Ideas	14
Triage and Prioritize	15
Capturing New Ideas to Drive Innovation	15
The Role of Enterprise Architecture in the Strategic Planning Process	15
EA in the Strategic Planning Lifecycle	17
"Do the Right Things"	17
"Do Things Right"	17
Types of Enterprise Architect	18
WHAT IS INNOVATION MANAGEMENT?	**19**
Overview	19
Innovation Campaigns	20
Innovation Journeys	20
Innovation Scorecards	21
Innovation management process	21
WHAT IS AGILE ENTERPRISE ARCHITECTURE?	**23**
Overview	23
An agile approach to enterprise architecture	23
Just in time EA	23
Just enough EA	24
Consistency vs. Just Enough	24
Business Agility	25
ENTERPRISE ARCHITECTURE FRAMEWORKS	**27**
Overview	27
What is enterprise architecture?	27
Types of enterprise architecture framework	28
Meta-models	29

Summary	30
COMMUNITIES	**31**
Overview	31
Summary	32
COLLABORATION	**33**
Agile techniques	33
Kanban and Innovation Management	35
Kanban and Enterprise Architecture	38
Using Kanban as a mechanism for EA change	41
Kanban and Agility	41
Tasks	43
Tasks, Innovation Management and Enterprise Architecture	44
Collaboration summary	45
GAMIFICATION	**47**
Overview	47
Detail and techniques	47
Summary	50
MODELS AND VIEWS	**51**
Overview	51
Views	52
ROADMAPPING	**57**
Overview	57
Enterprise Architecture Roadmaps	57
Summary	61
ANALYTICS AND DECISION MAKING	**63**
Overview	63
Analytical Hierarchy Process (Pairwise Comparison)	63
Charts and infographics	66
Pivot tables	73
Heatmaps	74
Scorecards	74
Summary	77
WORK PACKAGES AND PROJECTS	**79**
Overview	79
Detail and techniques	81

Summary	84

WORKSPACES AND VERSIONING — 87

Overview	87
Detail and techniques	87
Dealing with change	87
Merge and extract	91
Summary	94

PORTFOLIO MANAGEMENT — 95

Overview	95
Measuring portfolio performance	97
Net Present Value (NPV)	97
Summary	98

IDEAS TO DELIVERY — 99

Overview	99
How does an organization successfully embrace change?	99
Agile Development and DevOps	101

CREATING A BUSINESS CASE — 107

Overview	107
A business case should be agile	108
Summary	117

CENTRE OF EXCELLENCE — 119

Overview	119
Example of Return on Investment	122

FINAL SUMMARY — 125

Strategic Planning Platform	125
A Federated View Of Data	126
Customization is important	126

Analytical Hierarchy Process (AHP) Example — 127

Using AHP	127
Decision making with AHP	138

ArchiMate 2.1 Reference Guide — 139

Organization Viewpoint	139
Actor Co-operation Viewpoint	140
Business Function Viewpoint	141

Business Process Co-operation Viewpoint	141
Business Process Viewpoint	142
Product Viewpoint	142
Application Behavior Viewpoint	143
Application Co-operation Viewpoint	143
Application Structure Viewpoint	144
Application Usage Viewpoint	144
Infrastructure Viewpoint	145
Infrastructure Usage Viewpoint	145
Implementation and Deployment Viewpoint	146
Information Structure Viewpoint	146
Service Realization Viewpoint	147
Layered Viewpoint	148
Stakeholder Viewpoint	149
Goal Realization Viewpoint	149
Goal Contribution Viewpoint	150
Principles Viewpoint	150
Requirements Realization Viewpoint	150
Motivation Viewpoint	151
Project Viewpoint	152
Migration Viewpoint	152
Implementation and Migration Viewpoint	153
Business Capability Viewpoint	154
Business Capability Increment Viewpoint	154
Idea to Delivery Viewpoint	155
Capability to Application Component Viewpoint	155
Meta-type to Viewpoint Matrix	156
ArchiMate Concepts	157
Core Meta-model	158
Meta-model extensions	159
References	160

FOREWARD

Traditional Innovation Management best practices have often stopped at the implementation phase. So you've prioritized your organizations best ideas - now what?

Enterprise Architecture, which is where the business and IT infrastructure is captured and analyzed, has struggled to communicate its value and prioritize its initiatives.

Both of these areas have rarely been connected or managed together.

At the same time, agile principles have moved from an approach used by cutting edge software development teams to being the standard approach adopted by teams large and small.

In this book, we bring all three of these disciplines together so that they each add value to one another and can help in any of the following:

- Enterprise wide innovation management
- Goal oriented innovation management
- Value driven enterprise architecture
- Business agility
- Collaborative ideation and delivery (including DevOps)
- Application portfolio management
- Project or program management
- Capability assessment and management

A structured yet agile approach allows organizations to concentrate on innovation that can be realized through enterprise architecture. Agile techniques provide collaboration and focus to these initiatives.

ABOUT THIS BOOK

Welcome to Agile Enterprise Architecture and Innovation Management. You've probably been hearing about Agile, Enterprise Architecture and Innovation Management for some time which isn't surprising as they are all important disciplines in their own right.

If you've not been exposed to any of these or not used these together, then this book is here to help.

There are differing levels of content in this book, and we've chosen to either describe a topic and why it is relevant or deep dive into the topic when we think it's necessary.

You will also notice different styles in this book. It's written pragmatically using best practices we've collected over the years, and of course, involves Martin and Alan's different writing styles!

This book will not attempt to show you how to do enterprise architecture or innovation management, but provides a tool kit of techniques that our clients have found beneficial over the past 20 years.

ASSUMPTIONS

Many people and teams can benefit most from this book, but we took the liberty to assume the following:

- You're looking at supporting some form of innovation in your organization. Whether you're a business owner, architect, line of business manager, process owner or have some other role, you would like to understand how to capture innovation.

- You may have used enterprise architecture in the past but couldn't appreciate, extract or demonstrate the value of it within your organization.

- You've had some success and you're looking to grow your innovation management and/or enterprise architecture practice.

- You want to try combining agile techniques with enterprise architecture best practices to achieve better agility.

- You want to use innovation management and enterprise architecture in conjunction with each other but are unsure of the benefits or approach.

- You would like to see how enterprise architecture could be more closely aligned project delivery.

AUTHORS

MARTIN OWEN

Martin has held executive and senior management and technical positions in IBM, Telelogic and Popkin. He has been instrumental in driving forward the product management of enterprise architecture, portfolio management and asset management tooling.

Martin is also active with industry standards bodies and was the driver behind the first business process-modeling notation (BPMN) standard.

Martin has led the ArchiMate® and UML mapping initiatives at the Open Group and is part of the capability based planning standards team.

Martin is responsible for strategy, products and direction at Corso.

ALAN BURNETT

Alan has held senior technical and managerial positions at IBM, Telelogic and Popkin and is responsible for worldwide consulting at Corso.

Alan has been managing enterprise architecture product implementations for over 20 years and has built up an extensive knowledge of what is required in order for these to be successful.

Alan has implemented communities of excellence around enterprise architecture and innovation at many of the world's leading organizations.

Alan is part of the ArchiMate® and TOGAF® harmonization team at the Open Group.

SPECIAL THANKS

Putting this book together took a lot of work. Although Martin and Alan are the main authors, there are many people that have helped to get this book out, including:

Leigh Weston, Jon Lederer, Nick Milbourn, Dan Aston, Paul Banim, Aidan Kelly, Alan Batchelder, Kingsley Pinto, Oliver Bell and Wendy Higgins

A special thanks to the Corso development team (our team of millennials!) who have come up with many great ideas throughout the development of our EA and innovation management software. Often coming up with ideas we hadn't even thought about when we started Corso!

OUR SOFTWARE

A driver behind this book is to put down into words the knowledge we've gained over many years and to build a software platform based upon these techniques.

Therefore, you will see references to technology and our platform in this book.

Our software was built from the ground up. Having been involved in enterprise architecture product management and development at Popkin software, Telelogic and then IBM, we had a good idea of what we wanted to build and how we wanted to change the market perception of EA and innovation management. That definitely included changing the price perception of these types of tools.

The time was right from a market and technology perspective to design and build our platform.

We've used the latest software development tools and techniques in the building of the platform and are constantly leading and putting cutting edge capabilities together.

All of the techniques described in this book are supported by our platform. We anticipate putting further revisions of this book together as we expand our capabilities.

At the time of printing this book, we've already expanded the capabilities of the platform considerably based on customer feedback and our rapid development approach.

CHAPTER 1

AGILE EA AND INNOVATION MANAGEMENT OVERVIEW

In a corporate sense, innovation management is about quickly and effectively implementing your organization goals through the adoption of innovative ideas, products, processes and business models. Most organizations are beginning to realize that to drive business growth and maintain a competitive advantage, innovation needs to be discovered and implemented quickly and with care to ensure maximum value.

The process of innovation needs to be managed and governed in the organization and is an important facet of a company's overall function.

Enterprise architecture (EA) is a perennial tool for innovation. This is because once you develop a good idea, you need to ensure that EA is leveraged and to begin to understand how to implement it successfully. Investment in a particular idea requires a degree of confidence that a product, service, IT component or business process is going to make it to market or change the business positively. Conversely, IT requires traceability back to the innovation that has driven it. Not having this traceability means that it's difficult to see the value of IT and how it drives the business. Additionally, there is a need to leverage the limited interaction between those who innovate and those who manage EA.

Without EA, decision-making expanding from the right ideas and requirements is much more of a lottery. And, while there are more and more projects in progress and a rise in agile development approaches, companies simply do not invest enough time in combining innovation and EA. DevOps and continuous delivery are prime candidates for connection into innovation management. In the context of speed and time to market, where the frequency, capability and release cycles are key to competitive advantage, EA's support of decision-making allows innovative ideas to be implemented without costly mistakes.

THE IMPORTANCE OF AN AGILE APPROACH TO ENTERPRISE ARCHITECTURE

Enterprise architecture has often failed when it's targeted at modeling the entire enterprise. So performing the appropriate amount of enterprise architecture is required to achieve results. Agile Enterprise Architecture is an approach that assists us in reigning in the constant temptation to build the perfect architecture.

I'm sure you know what that perfect architecture is? It involves months, often years, of development, it includes every possible perspective, view, layer, horizontal, and vertical slice and dice. Analysis paralysis. And we're still waiting to find a stakeholder to champion it, let alone someone from business to gain value from it and promote it.

It's our classic waterfall development approach. We don't want to actually build anything until we're 100% sure we've captured every requirement and designed it to within an ounce of its life. We've all been brought up on the metrics that tell us how much it costs to change something once we're in development, versus when we're in design. And, guess what, business transformation moves faster than that these days, so enterprise architecture needs to keep pace.

Agile approaches such as Scrum can sometimes be used to build small pieces of enterprise architecture delivering exactly what is needed. Scrum techniques harness team working, delivery in time slots and identifying 'experts' to help with specific issues.

Other techniques such as 'Kanban' can be used to help visualize the status of architectural concepts and their journey in the agile process. In innovation management we can show users the journey of different concepts in the innovation lifecycle, which improves the visibility for the whole team. When coupled with EA frameworks such as ArchiMate® and TOGAF®, Scrum provides the focus to EA.

An Agile approach to EA allows for continuous improvement and ties nicely to incremental ideas that the business receives.

LINKING INNOVATION MANAGEMENT AND ENTERPRISE ARCHITECTURE

We've noticed that EA thinking is not influencing innovation management in the way it should be because innovation projects are not necessarily aligned with the transformational needs of the business. Enterprise Architecture is typically addressing transformational challenges such as mergers/acquisitions, business and IT alignment, adoption of big data, IT outsourcing etc. There are too many ideas and many more projects than there needs to be.

EA needs to find a place to influence innovation management. Where innovation is growing, EA provides just enough architecture to help influence innovation decision making and current innovation management platforms have not addressed EA.

It's an oversight but it is understandable as the heritage of these older platforms do not provide the rigour needed for an EA approach. Organizations resources are scarce, so it's absolutely crucial that we make use of the resources in a way that benefits everyone. With Innovation Management and EA, we can help companies do this by providing them with guidance in selecting the right course of action from the resources available. Consequently, a platform that can marry innovation management and agile EA can provide true decision making for innovation initiatives and EA activities.

Innovation needs to be real and linking it to the underlying enterprise architecture demonstrates how ideas have evolved. Enterprise Architecture needs to be able to address real innovation. If the architecture changes what effect does this have on innovation and its related strategies?

Innovation Management and Agile Enterprise Architecture go hand in hand. Although each can be successful in their own right, it's when they are used in conjunction with each other that the full benefits can be realized.

CHAPTER 2

MANAGING CHANGE IN A TECHNOLOGICAL WORLD

OVERVIEW

Today's business world is driven by constant change. Organizations that embrace change as a constant often achieve greater success. The majority of changes to any business will require changes to its technology. Organizations often succeed or fail based on choosing the right technologies to help them embrace change, then using them in the right way. Ensuring that the right changes are made and the impact of those changes is well understood in advance of execution is vital. While good ideas help the business grow, their implementations have caused many a company to stumble.

Organizations face two major hurdles when adopting change, especially changes that are linked to technology. First, employees often don't have a structured mechanism to submit ideas that would improve the company and help it reach its goals. The ideas often disappear into a black hole. Employees don't get feedback on the viability of their idea or whether it will be adopted. The result? A reduced incentive to innovate.

Secondly, a disconnect can often occur between the idea or innovation and its implementation. Delivery, or incorporation of the new ideas into daily operations using technology often gets pushed aside or considered as an afterthought. The result? Redundancies in technology and processes, the inefficient use of resources and a missed opportunity.

In large organizations, enterprise architecture (EA) has long been recognized as an effective mechanism for assessing the impact of change on an organization and making recommendations for target states that support its business objectives. New solution architectures are also being used to successfully assess solution alternatives to support these target states.

While EA often delivers the businesses cases that justify the incorporation of ideas into operations, in reality, the EA function often still operates in an ivory tower. The group is often disconnected from the stakeholders as well as the IT projects team assigned to deliver the solution. While the EA teams develop business cases that link the change to the greater corporate strategies, the team can suffer from a lack of commitment from the wider organization. EA team recommendations are often ignored. As a result, ideas are adopted without the rigorous scrutiny of the idea, its execution and impact on other projects.

What's needed is an integrated approach that marries the EA team's knowledge with a process for managing ideas and innovation. A strategic planning approach -- from assessment and impact and investment analysis through to delivery--ensures ideas are being captured, analyzed and shared in a structured process. Feedback goes back to the originator and the right stakeholders are involved in making the right decisions about IT projects using sound business cases. This leads to both the stakeholder community and the EA community feeling empowered to make change.

A strategic planning platform brings a federated view of information from across the organization so that it can be shared. The platform is designed to help organizations analyze and prioritize ideas, feed them into enterprise architecture for analysis and compile into a business case. With all stakeholders reviewing the information and providing feedback on proposed projects, everyone gets a voice. It gives organizations the means to systematically manage change and provide an integrated platform for everyone to understand how new ideas fit into the corporate strategy. Not only that, this process can be executed in near real-time, allowing the organization to react quickly to seize market advantage.

COLLECTING & HARVESTING NEW IDEAS

Today, organizations are bombarded with new ideas, from all departments, levels and the operating environment. Many of the ideas, especially those with real merit, get lost because the organization lacks a formal structure for capturing and analyzing them.

Social media tools on phones, tablets and other portable and desktop devices offer tremendous opportunities to most organizations. Tools such as Twitter, LinkedIn, Facebook and Yammer have brought a new expectation for the speed and capture of communications between people. The line has blurred between personal and business as these tools become more woven into our culture.

As mobile devices proliferate and more people access these platforms, organizations are looking for ways to capture and adopt new ideas. Tools like Yammer can be used to capture and filter ideas from employees, customers and partners. In the same vein, employees can use these tools to more easily connect to the heart of the organization and feel empowered to contribute. These tools can help make sense of incoming data without losing the speed of capturing and processing it. Techniques such as the ubiquitous "I like this" thumb found on Facebook can act as powerful mechanisms to monitor the approval of peer groups.

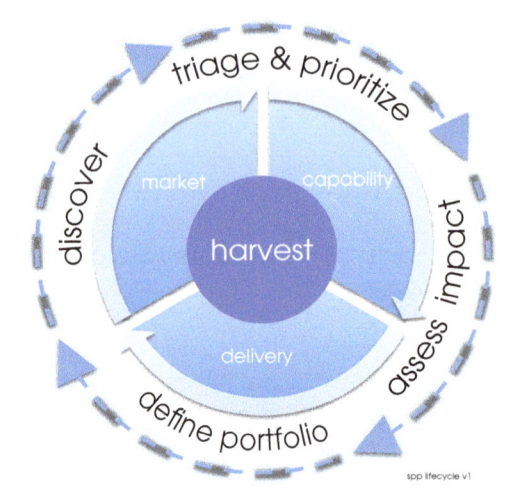

More importantly, these tools are the first step to enable different groups—PMO, IT, EA, Operations--to gather and share information through the entire idea lifecycle--from the capture of an idea through its implementation.

TRIAGE AND PRIORITIZE

Organizations could harness social media tools to provide a public 'idea' portal for quickly harvesting innovation or they could use an innovation management tool. This raw feed of ideas then requires triaging and prioritizing. An initial assessment can be made with three potential outcomes: (1) not appropriate or otherwise rejected; (2) need more information; and (3) ready to be seriously evaluated.

Capture is followed by triage—prioritizing and analyzing the ideas quickly and with minimal resources. At this point, ideas can be assigned for further assessment or rejected for practical purposes, due to laws, competitive factors, resource limitations, costs or other reasons.

In addition to harvesting ideas using social media tools, organizations can gather market information for assessment purposes. These tools can harvest data from a wide range of sources, such as CRM platforms, external databases and other industry sources. The assessment team can use these resources to quickly look at marketing, financial or industry factors to determine which ideas would deliver most value at least risk and cost to the organization.

Social media tools also enable a feedback loop. By establishing a central ideas portal, employees who propose ideas can view their status at any time. Reward schemes can further stimulate innovation and idea submission. By creating this loop, employees can see the value of their ideas and feel more empowered to suggest other ways to innovate.

CAPTURING NEW IDEAS TO DRIVE INNOVATION

In many organizations, new ideas are captured via a simple, but silo-oriented process. They are submitted, then reviewed by an independent Program Management Board (owned by the program management office (PMO)) which is controlled by the Chief Information Officer (CIO). The PMO decides on both the projects and the funding. In some cases, the EA team may be asked to review the idea and provide feedback, including business cases and transition plans. The PMO reviews this data, then hands approved projects and changes to IT for implementation. Each step in the process is performed independently; each area uses its own set of tools to analyze the data. This limits what data can be and is shared and reinforces organizational silos.

While this approach has sometimes worked in the past, it makes organization-wide strategic planning difficult if not impossible. The capture, analysis and approval of ideas are almost always managed separately from their implementation with little visibility among those involved. Organizations can't trace the process from collection through implementation. Business cases may not be part of the formal process. In organizations with a large portfolio of projects it becomes difficult to assess how new ideas affect the existing project portfolio. Questions arise, such as will this idea need us to terminate or change an existing project? Is there already a planned project that may deliver a similar result? Is there a new project that will be affected? Who do we need to ask to find this out?

THE ROLE OF ENTERPRISE ARCHITECTURE IN THE STRATEGIC PLANNING PROCESS

Identifying and analyzing new ideas across the organization is the first step in the strategic planning process of successful organizations. While portfolio management and the PMO evaluate the initial idea, the EA team evaluates ideas with top priority and compiles a business case for pursuing (or not pursuing) the idea. The team examines whether the new idea contradicts or extends existing projects. It examines risk, time schedules, effects on corporate goals and how the changes would be constrained by the principles and controls of the organization. It develops transition plans and suggests solution alternatives that describe the impact of the change, including estimates on cost, risk, resources, etc.

The business case is shared across the PMO, IT, portfolio management and the business teams to help them make an informed decision about whether to pursue the idea for implementation. A review board can regularly review returned business cases, prioritize them based on a range of objective and subjective factors such as cost, financial return, strategic relevance, opinions of stakeholders and risk. Business cases are then translated

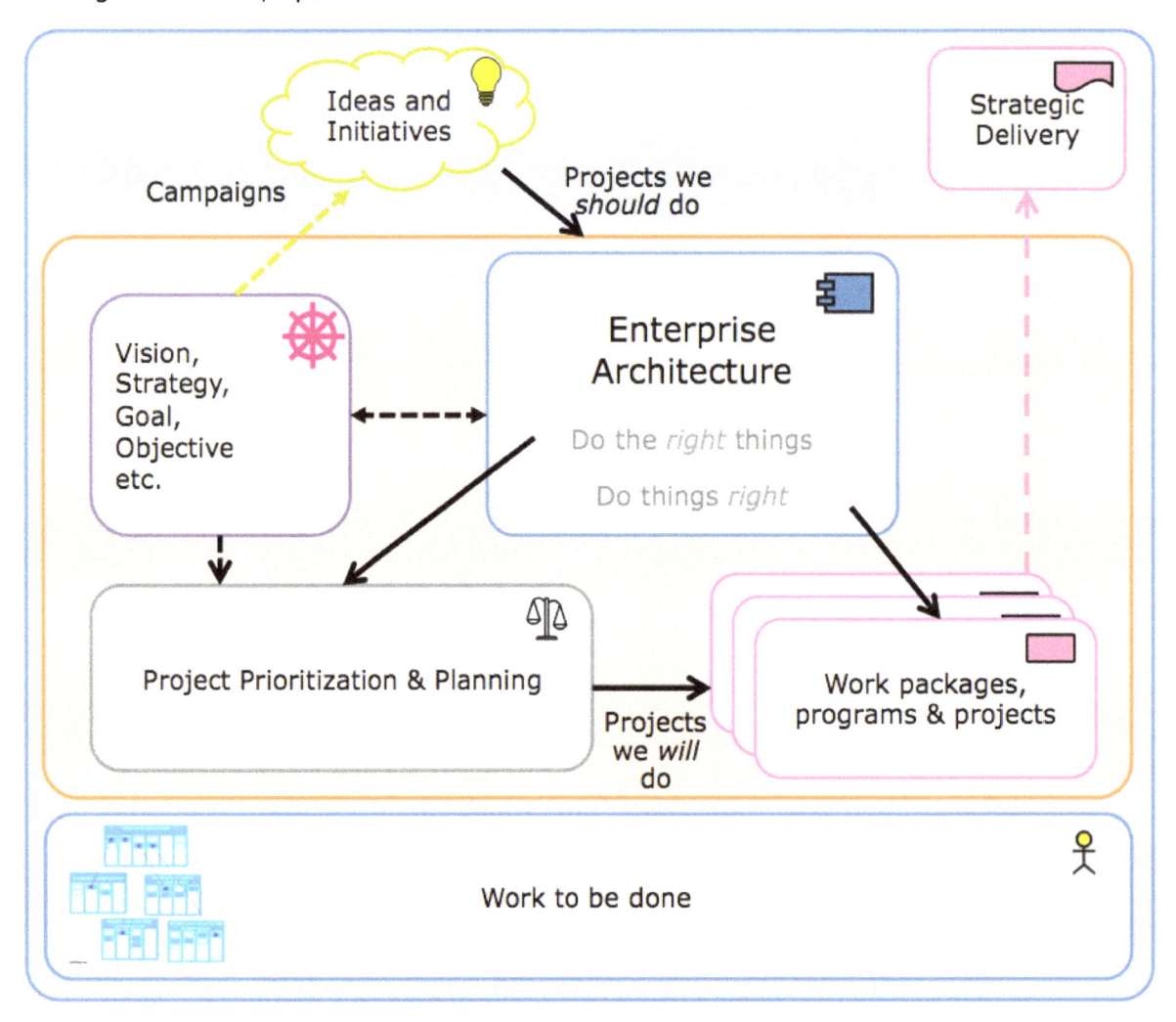

Figure 1: Strategic planning lifecycle

into initiatives and projects, which can be scheduled for execution.

EA IN THE STRATEGIC PLANNING LIFECYCLE

EA is often seen as bringing an 'ivory tower' perspective in the adoption of new ideas. But, in the context of this new, integrated approach to strategic planning, the EA function becomes more integrated within the organization and more focused on clearly defined objectives. The EA lifecycle process is based on the belief that the purpose of an EA is to focus on how to "Do the right things" and "Do things right."

"DO THE RIGHT THINGS"

The EA team compiles and analyses structured information on the:

Internal capabilities of the organization, goals and long term strategies these capabilities support, and resources that support the goals and strategies.

The EA team reviews high priority initiatives against the capabilities and resources they affect. Initial analysis can be made on the impact of new initiatives on existing projects and whether they are in line with existing strategy.

Target state architectures can be built which deliver the details around each initiative. From these, solution alternatives assess costs, resource estimates and risk. The result is a well-defined business case for that initiative.

In developing a business case, the EA team brings together silos of information from various resources, both internal and external, to sort out singular and overlapping ideas. Analysis helps sharpen the focus on key information and provide knowledge in a useful context. This approach helps the PMO to make smarter decisions about allocating funding and resources to projects. The business case also gives stakeholders such as IT a voice in the process before it reaches the implementation stage. EA's role is to synthesize the information in such a way that it helps the organization focus on doing the right things and ensuring they are done the right way.

"DO THINGS RIGHT"

The EA team also plays a long-term strategic role. An EA can hold information about past successes and reusable assets such as patterns along with a library of guiding principles agreed by the organization. As new projects begin, a clear high-level overview of what the project will deliver along with any patterns and principles that must apply will be presented. In this manner, the EA acts in a governance role to ensure reuse of investment and standardization is maintained. The improved control reduces risk and cost. As projects conclude, the output of the project will be assessed and reusable assets harvested into the architectural asset library. This provides a historical context for future decisions.

TYPES OF ENTERPRISE ARCHITECT

Today's EA practitioners fall into two primary roles:

- Vanguard enterprise architect
- Foundational enterprise architect

An innovation driver, the vanguard architect deals with technology disruptions and enterprise connectivity, while the foundational enterprise architect maintains enterprise technology and the systems of record.

The vanguard practitioner is emerging as a person with an ability to make and communicate business decisions that transcend digital business and technological disrupters. Gartner predicts the number of these practitioners will grow considerably.

The vanguard enterprise architect is an agile role by nature, dealing with constant innovation and change.

The future of EA puts the enterprise architect in a leadership role by driving strategy based on business goals and drivers. Deliverables for this emerging breed of enterprise architect include strategic guidance from the CxO-suite and downwards using the innovation and EA tools described in this book.

The diverse skill set of this version of the enterprise architect links digital business, social connectedness, and technology.

To build out these types of teams, organizations are looking to the millennial generation who have garnered these skills due to early exposure to technology and the digital world.

This is not to say that historical knowledge of EA practices and an understanding of modeling and IT structures is no longer valued, but skill sets need to evolve with business requirements. The new face of EA will succeed through fresh, big picture thinking combined with traditional application of models and data.

Today's reality is that pretty much any capability the business innovates will require the technology department to figure out how to deliver it and at speed. This means an understanding of how this technology will not only impact its users, but the entire business ecosystem will be a highly valued contribution to the enterprise and the vanguard enterprise architect is very well positioned to deliver that value.

CHAPTER 3

WHAT IS INNOVATION MANAGEMENT?

OVERVIEW

Innovation management is the management of innovation processes. It refers both to organizational and product innovation. Innovation management includes a set of techniques and tools that allow managers and engineers to cooperate with a common understanding of processes and goals.

It has always been the mission of executives to foster innovation in the work place. In the past, large companies have relied on out-dated and under-used suggestion boxes, spreadsheets or poorly functioning software to harvest ideas from their stakeholders. Until now, these shortcomings have largely remained unanswered and unsolvable.

Historically, Innovation management tools were generally limited to aid companies in focussing their idea contributors on specific goals. To compound this problem further, tooling was generally geared towards a single user, rather than the enterprise itself. Unfortunately, this did not eliminate the need for the suggestion box despite moderate improvements in our ability to innovate.

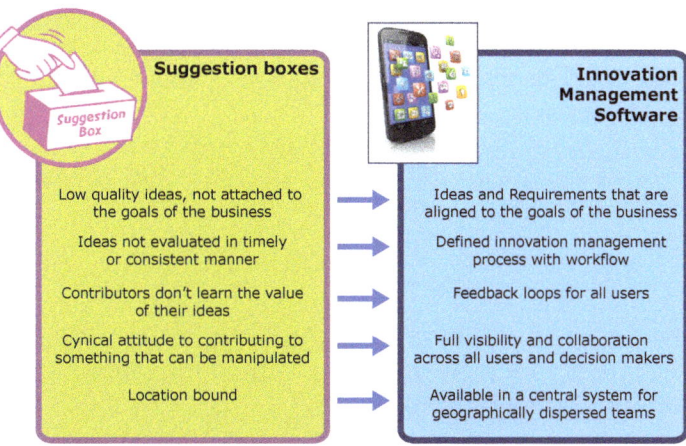

Suggestion boxes	Innovation Management Software
Low quality ideas, not attached to the goals of the business	Ideas and Requirements that are aligned to the goals of the business
Ideas not evaluated in timely or consistent manner	Defined innovation management process with workflow
Contributors don't learn the value of their ideas	Feedback loops for all users
Cynical attitude to contributing to something that can be manipulated	Full visibility and collaboration across all users and decision makers
Location bound	Available in a central system for geographically dispersed teams

Figure 2: Suggestion box to Innovation Management

One of the biggest complaints to this day is that suggestion box users almost never see their ideas come to fruition. Fast-forward to today, Innovation Management is powered by its users, who can set up and manage a closed-loop evaluation process. The beauty of this kind of automation is that it seeks to eliminate contributors' reluctance to submit after a previous idea hasn't been followed up. The evolution has allowed users to be automatically reminded of upcoming deadlines and unevaluated ideas.

The same applies to online/offline survey methods. For example, Survey Monkey allows an idea to be submitted but doesn't give the user a sense of visibility and collaboration in the ideation process. There's a similar theme with other antiquated methods like postal surveys. The Innovation revolution has made these kinds of methods obsolete in a forward thinking business environment.

Have you ever felt like it's impossible to measure the ROI of your Knowledge Management (KM) system? The evolution of Ideas Management tooling is now sharing some common ground with KM. Ideas Management doesn't seek to replace KM, only to supplement it in a way that works for the business. Why not pair up your knowledge, expertise and wisdom with your ideas, proposals and theories?

INNOVATION CAMPAIGNS

The ideation process has evolved so that users can set up 'campaigns' as part of their innovation strategy. Users can use campaigns to ask a community for specific ideas to solve a particular business problem or to encourage innovation around a specific topic. Marketing relies on a framework called the Marketing Mix and a similar kind of framework can be applied to a campaign in Innovation Management. For example, Ideation can now be targeted to a specific department, job title or even age range. Narrowing the population allows users to gain a more filtered selection of ideas, ideas that are more relevant - the cream of the crop.

Example:

> "The Central Bean Coffee Co. is a growing start-up that provides mobile coffee services to other companies. It has offices in Birmingham UK, Melbourne Australia and New York in the US. The company is extremely lean and relies on its employees and customers to contribute ideas that will enable the organization to perform better. The company wants to know what services it can offer during 2016 that will grow their customers' use of the service.
>
> The company will run a campaign throughout 2015/16 that will collect ideas."

INNOVATION JOURNEYS

What is exciting is the introduction of Kanban. This evolution within ideas management has allowed users to track ideas from their inception to their implementation and Kanban helps to visualize, organize and complete these ideas.

The first official use of Kanban can be traced back to Taiichi Ohno's work at Toyota. He needed a way to quickly communicate to all workers how much work was being done, what state it was in and how the work was progressing. His goal was to make information and processes transparent to everybody and not just the management team. With Innovation Management we've taken the concept of Kanban a step further and allow users to show the journey of concepts therefore improving visibility for the whole team. What's more, Kanban boards are completely customizable. Clients can alter existing board structures or add completely new types of board.

INNOVATION SCORECARDS

With innovation management you need to be able to track key metrics in a way that is useful not only to a stakeholder but also to Directors and Shareholders. Using scorecards (discussed later in this book), you are able to calculate value, or estimate the savings made and the revenue generated by a particular idea. You can calculate ROI with ease, without the use of over complicated spreadsheets that only one person can interpret and own.

We've come a long way since the days of putting pieces of paper in a box. Do away with your nostalgia; this is the evolution of Ideas Management!

INNOVATION MANAGEMENT PROCESS

A major theme within ideation is the **managed innovation management process** (as shown in Figure 3).

The process shows a funnel that manages how an idea can materialize into a new service or product through the managed innovation process. In an ideal environment, innovation champions (catalysts), business sponsors and managers help move and refine the ideas through the process. The funnel acts as mechanism in which the best ideas are fully vetted and brought to market at the end of the process.

However, the innovation funnel should not be used in isolation. The process works best when other stakeholders such as enterprise architects and portfolio managers are involved.

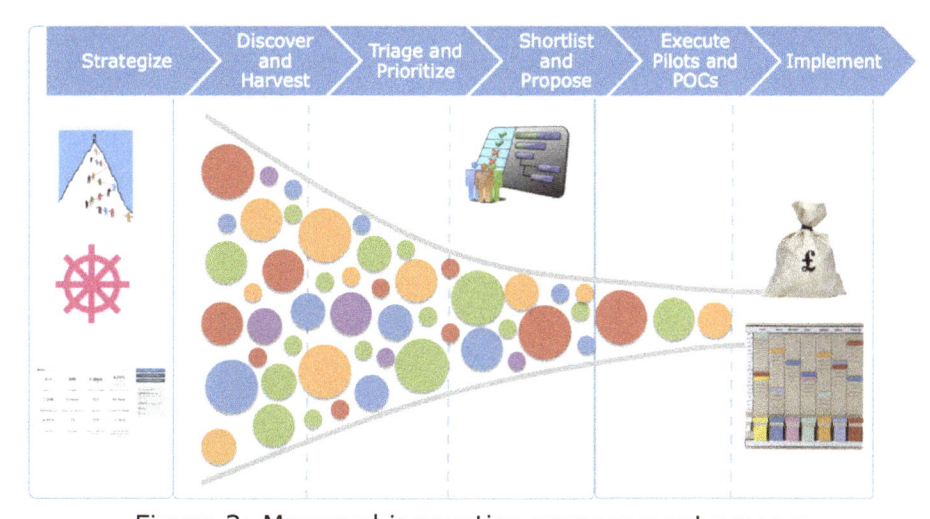

Figure 3: Managed innovation management process

CHAPTER 4

WHAT IS AGILE ENTERPRISE ARCHITECTURE?

OVERVIEW

Undoubtedly, there is a need for organizations to embrace enterprise architecture (EA). How else would you be able to change and respond to business and IT needs without first of all writing down what you have, want and need?

The old adage that anything of any complexity needs to be modelled before it can be changed definitely holds true. The issue, is that enterprise architects have tended to model everything down to an excruciating level of detail, often getting lost in the weeds and rarely surfacing for air to see what the rest of the business is doing, and realizing what it needs.

Ask yourself this question; has EA got a bad reputation for not providing any business value except for a wall covering of designs?

Frameworks and languages such as TOGAF®, ArchiMate® and DODAF aren't responsible for this perception. In fact, these standards provide a mechanism for communication and delivery, but it's how enterprise architects have used them in the past that brings issues.

AN AGILE APPROACH TO ENTERPRISE ARCHITECTURE

We've all heard the terms "just in time", "just enough", "agile development and delivery" - but how do these affect EA? What's missing in EA is the delivery of '*just in time*' and doing '*just enough*' architecture to achieve results. It's time the EA team met the desires of stakeholders by only doing enough of what is required to meet those expectations. Sometimes, a deeper EA initiative is required such as in defence projects or on large complex programs, and 'just enough' may not have the rigour or depth that you require.

JUST IN TIME EA

Agile is based on "just in time". You can see this in many of the agile practices, especially in DevOps. User stories are created when they are needed and not before and releases happen when there is appropriate value in releasing, not before and not after. Additionally, each iteration has a commitment that is met on time by the EA team.

JUST ENOUGH EA

EA is missing the answer to the question; *what exactly is getting delivered?* This is where we introduce the phrase "just enough, just in time" because stakeholders don't just simply want it in time, they also want just enough of it – regardless of what *it* is!

This is especially important when communicating with non-EA professionals. In the past, enterprise architects have focussed on delivering all of the EA assets to stakeholders and demonstrating the technical wizardry required to build the actual architecture. Does this contribute to the demise of EA in the stakeholders' eyes?

Let's look at a few examples of techniques that help provide just enough enterprise architecture:

Campaigns - create a marketing style campaign to focus on EA initiatives. Focus on gathering and describing only what is required to satisfy the goal of the campaign.

Models - at the start of the project it doesn't make sense to build out a fancy EA, which is going to change anyway. Teams should be striving to build just enough architecture to support the campaigns in the pipeline.

Collaboration – agile teams certainly have high levels of collaboration, and that's because that level is just enough to help them be successful.

Planning – at iteration planning we don't look at things outside the iteration. We do just enough planning to make sure we can accomplish our goal for the iteration. Work packages and tasks play a large role in both planning and collaboration.

CONSISTENCY VS. JUST ENOUGH

Doing just enough doesn't mean that we should do this at the expense of consistency. After all, a big benefit of enterprise architecture is the ability to slice across the architecture for decision-making and 'what if' analysis. The underlying model should still be consistent and it should be described to a level of detail and consistency that makes it meaningful. **This is the skill of the agile enterprise architect.**

USEFUL EA TOOLS

Light sketches and mindmaps are useful to brainstorm before getting into more formal modeling. Although not a formal part of architecture frameworks such as TOGAF® and ArchiMate®, they can provide a useful communication mechanism.

ArchiMate provides a standard notation and meta-model for EA but we certainly do not need to do all of it to achieve results from our architecture. However, ArchiMate® provides EA with a common language for communication and therefore ensuring consistency across our teams.

Socialization and gamification - involving other experts and communities in the EA effort provides the benefit of 'buy in'. Leader boards, likes and rewards are all mechanisms to reward stakeholders for their participation in the EA initiatives.

Collaboration - Tracking work and allowing team members to collaborate is critical, not only for EA teams. **The agile community has used Kanban boards** because they can be used to track tasks and issues for the team and also be used to show where facets of the EA are in the workload. Additionally, a Kanban can be used to 'force' progression of work so that it is completed on time.

Goal-based campaigns - In order to focus EA efforts, campaigns can be used to set a start and end date. Kanban, along with communities and tasks can all be geared around achieving goals in much the same way that a marketing campaign has end goals, metrics, and deliverables. A marketing campaign is ultimately measured by its success and similarly campaigns in Agile EA can be measured on success rate.

Publications/Documentation - We certainly do not need "just in case" documentation, but its crazy to think that agile teams can be effective without documentation. We need just enough documentation to make sure the team is successful.

Presentation slides - When information and architecture is changing rapidly, then documentation-led enterprise architecture is often at odds with just in time and just enough. Dynamic documentation or the ability to present information quickly and without fuss becomes paramount.

BUSINESS AGILITY

An agile approach to enterprise architecture is about enabling business agility, and this can be achieved through a variety of techniques and tools that support building architecture quickly and efficiently. Targeting a business goal and doing just enough architecture to achieve that goal helps an organization be more agile.

CHAPTER 5

ENTERPRISE ARCHITECTURE FRAMEWORKS

INTRODUCTION

This section explains what enterprise architecture frameworks are and how they fit into today's organizations. We cover the importance of enterprise architecture and why it is necessary.

OVERVIEW

In much the same way as any building or infrastructure project requires different stakeholders and different plan views, enterprise architecture requires the same.

You wouldn't build a house without understanding the building architecture, pipework's, electricity plans, ground plans, all within the context of each other.

Enterprise architecture provides the plans for different views of the enterprise. Enterprise architecture frameworks describe the standard views that an organization can expect to see.

WHAT IS ENTERPRISE ARCHITECTURE?

The discipline of enterprise architecture views an organization as an overall system of complex and intertwined systems.

Effective management of such complexity and scale requires tools and approaches that architects can use. An architecture framework provides the tools and approaches necessary to abstract this information to a level of detail that is manageable.

A framework helps bring enterprise design tasks into focus and produces valuable architecture description documentation.

The components of an architecture framework provide structured guidance that is divided into four main areas:

1. **Architecture description**: how to document the enterprise as a system from different viewpoints. Each view describes one domain of the architecture; it includes those meta-types and associations that address particular concerns of interest to particular stakeholders; it may take the form of a list, a table, a chart, a diagram, or a higher level of composite of such.

2. **Architecture notation**: how to visualize the enterprise in a standard manner. Each view can be represented by a standard depiction that is understandable and communicable to all stakeholders. One such notation is ArchiMate® from the open group.

3. **Design method**: processes that architects follow. Usually, an over arching enterprise architecture process, composed of phases, breaks into lower-level processes composed of finer grained activities. A process is defined by its objectives, inputs, phases (steps or activities) and outputs. Approaches, techniques, tools, principles, rules, and practices may support it. Agile architecture is one set of supporting techniques.

4. **Team organization**: guidance on the team structure, the governance of the team, the skills, experience and training needed. Kanban boards and agile architecture can help provide team structure, governance and best practice.

TYPES OF ENTERPRISE ARCHITECTURE FRAMEWORK

There are a number of popular enterprise architecture frameworks available, some follow:

ArchiMate - An Open Group Architecture Framework - a widely used framework that includes a notation for visualizing architecture. May be used in conjunction with TOGAF®.

TOGAF – The Open Group Architecture Framework – a widely used framework including an architectural Development Method and standards for describing various types of architecture.

DODAF - The Department of Defense Architecture Framework - the standard for defense architectures especially in the United States.

MODAF - The Ministry of Defense Architecture Framework - the UK standard for defense architectures.

NAF - the NATO Architecture Framework - a standard adopted for NATO allies.

FEAF - A federal enterprise architecture framework issued by the US Federal CIO council.

FEA - the 2002 Federal Enterprise Architecture (FEA) guidance on categorizing and grouping IT investments (issued by the US Federal Office of Management and Budget).

Zachman Framework - a classification scheme for EA artefacts launched in the early 1980s by John Zachman - often considered the father of Enterprise Architecture.

TM FORUM - Telemanagement forum - standard reference models for telecoms companies.

META-MODELS

A meta-model is a description of a classification of a set of things.

It describes the types of thing (meta-types), the rules between them (associations) and the attributes that describe them.

Meta-models can usually be built to describe any type of problem or scenario.

They are often graphical and are represented by boxes and lines. Boxes indicate the meta-types and lines represent the associations.

Meta-models are used by end users to express models.

In the Figure 4 meta-model example below, we could describe the relationship between a Pilot, Airline and Aircraft.

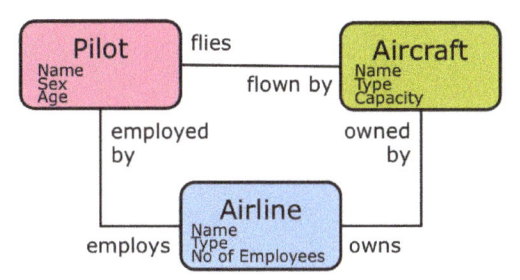

Figure 4: Meta-model

In the model in Figure 5 below, we use the meta-model to guide the construction of the model. The meta-model provides the framework within which the model can be constructed.

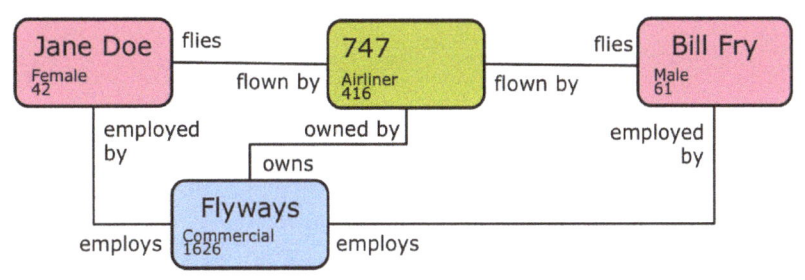

Figure 5: Model

In ArchiMate, the instances of the meta-types are called **Concepts**.

Each enterprise architecture framework will usually have an underlying meta-model that describes its meta-types and associations.

An example of a meta-model for innovation management is shown in Figure 6.

Further meta-models are shown at the back of this book.

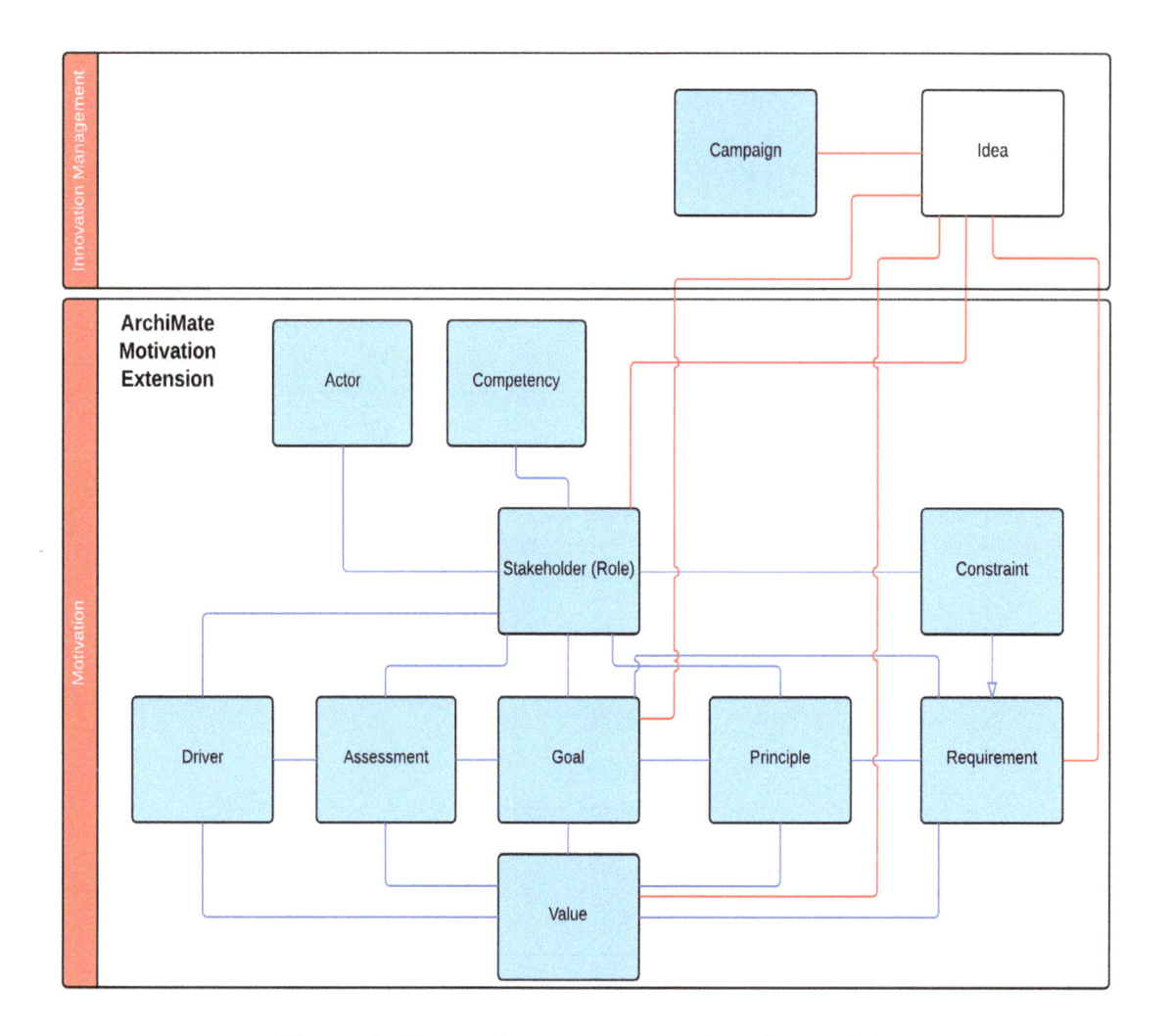

Figure 6: Innovation management meta-model

SUMMARY

This chapter covered the core concepts for meta-models and associations. Meta-models are the core building blocks for any architecture framework. They provide the basis for rigour and consistency for model data. Without a meta-model, the whole management of enterprise architecture and innovation management becomes extremely difficult.

CHAPTER 6

COMMUNITIES

INTRODUCTION

This chapter addresses communities and how they are organized to support enterprise architecture and innovation management initiatives.

Communities are vital in providing direction, views and access to concepts within organizations. They are formed from a particular viewpoint and normally contain members who have a similar interest. Usually administrators manage communities and in software tools they can have different visibility of concepts depending on their privileges.

OVERVIEW

Communities are a defined set of users that work together to achieve a common goal. Organizations have a need to manage different parts of their business in separate teams. For example, marketing ideas may need to be kept in marketing whereas HR ideas are kept in HR.

Communities allow companies to create identified groups of individuals or teams. Communities can then work on specific campaigns and concepts and discuss and share them in a private area where they are not visible to other platform users.

For large businesses, this is an excellent option for managing all of their concepts across multiple departments. An organization can also invite customers or suppliers to join specific groups to collaborate on ideas and innovation, to deliver shared benefits.

A member of a community may be designated a client administrator. A client administrator can add further members to the community and designate others as fellow administrators. It is important to think about communities from the outset of any initiative. Communities do not have to follow organization structure.

ROLES

Roles are an important concept. Each person in the organization may assume one or more roles. For example, a domain expert for a particular area may also have financial sign-off remit. Therefore that person may have the role of Business Analyst and Financial Approver.

Roles are important as most work in an organization is based on a role and not a person. This is also important where people move in and out of a company. The roles can remain the same. In ArchiMate, people and organizational units are known as Actors and Roles are roles.

STAKEHOLDERS

Stakeholders have an interest in the outcome of any initiative or objective of the community. They are a special type of Role. We identify them specifically as they are the roles that we need to make sure we are satisfying and are often associated with motivation aspects of an organization such as goals and drivers. The ArchiMate specification includes support for the modeling of stakeholder concerns.

PUBLIC, GATED AND PRIVATE COMMUNITIES

There are different types of community that may be recognized.

If you are using a software platform to manage your architecture and innovation, then the different community types control the access of communities to concepts within the platform.

Community Types

There are 3 types of community.

Public - anybody can join, they are available to everybody within a company to view and participate in.

Gated - anybody can see the name and description and can request to join

Private Only - hidden from anybody who is not a member

An organization could create a community for:

- Financial assessment of a set of ideas for a campaign. This may well be a private community.
- Development, which contains all development staff and development management.
- Product Management, which contains product marketing and the product manager.

SUMMARY

Communities provide the perfect mechanism to organize groups of people with a similar interest or goal. Community members will collaborate within their circles and will rapidly allow an organization to communicate in a better manner.

CHAPTER 7

COLLABORATION

INTRODUCTION

Collaboration is important for any organization undertaking innovation management and enterprise architecture initiatives.

Invariably you will be working as part of a team and you will need to communicate and garner feedback from other stakeholders in the organization.

AGILE TECHNIQUES

Agile techniques were born as a result of the failure of the dominant traditional software development project management paradigms (including waterfall lifecycle). It borrows many principles from lean manufacturing. In 2001, 17 pioneers of similar methods met at the Snowbird Ski Resort in Utah and wrote the Agile Manifesto, a declaration of four values and twelve principles. The Agile Manifesto placed a new emphasis on communication and collaboration, functioning software, team self-organization, and the flexibility to adapt to emerging business realities.

There are many agile techniques that conform to the agile manifesto.

These include Extreme Programming, Feature Driven Development, Dynamic Systems Development Method (DSDM), Scrum, and others.

These principles are fundamental to quick changing organizations and reflect well in the world we live in today. What's more, these techniques are critical to organizations that adopt innovation management and enterprise architecture with the end goal of better business agility.

KANBAN

Kanban boards are the visual storyboard for a process or workflow. They represent the journey and the concepts within that journey. Concepts are represented as cards on the board. Concepts may be moved from one stage to another by dragging a concept.

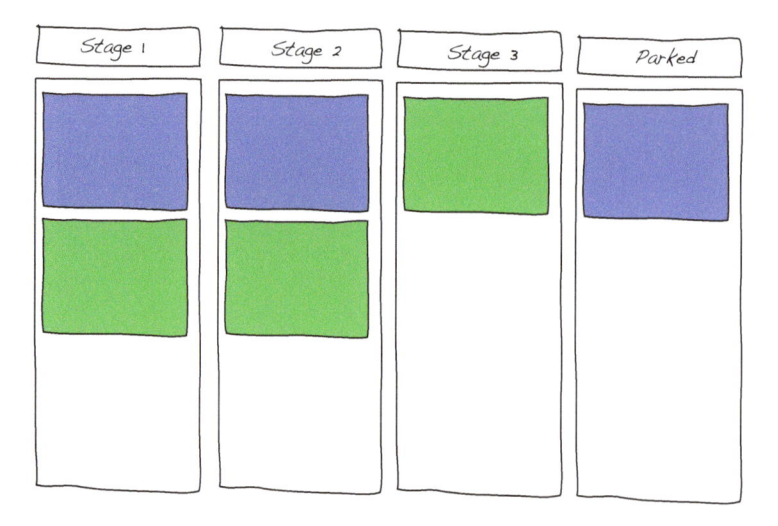

Figure 7:Kanban board

Kanban boards are based on the concept of Kanban. A Kanban is a tool to visualize, organize and complete work. The first official use of Kanban can be traced back to Taiichi Ohno's work at Toyota. He needed a way to quickly communicate to all workers how much work was being done, what state it was in and how the work was progressing. His goal was to make information and processes transparent to everybody and not just the management team.

Kanban can be user to allow users to show the journey of concepts through your processes, therefore improving visibility for the whole team.

What's more, the Kanban boards are completely customizable. They can alter existing board structures or add completely new types of board.

Following are some example Kanban boards:

Innovation Management - Provides a journey through innovation management.

Ideas Roadmap - Provides a roadmap by quarter of where ideas are likely to be released.

Ideas Management - Provides a journey of the status of ideas on a simple task board.

Requirements Management - Visualizes requirements over a development Kanban.

Feature Management - Shows where a set of features are in the development process.

Skills Management - Provides a view of what skills training is required to be planned.

Stages

A Kanban board is composed of stages. Stages are the placeholders for status of work and contain concepts. Depending upon the Kanban board that you are using, different types of concept may be present on a stage.

Limits

Each stage may be defined with a limit. A limit provides a maximum count for the number of concepts that can exist on a stage at any one time. This prevents a stage from being overloaded with too much work.

The use of stages also allows the Kanban process to be streamlined. The use of limits in various stages can force concepts along a pipeline and ensure that current work is complete before more work is added to a stage. Usually Kanban boards have administrators that may define the stages and limits on a Kanban.

KANBAN AND INNOVATION MANAGEMENT

As discussed previously, Innovation management has a funnel that supports taking an idea from initial concept to delivery.

The overall ideation process starts with a broad range of ideas and gradually refines and selects from them, creating a handful of formal development projects that can be pushed to rapid completion and introduction.

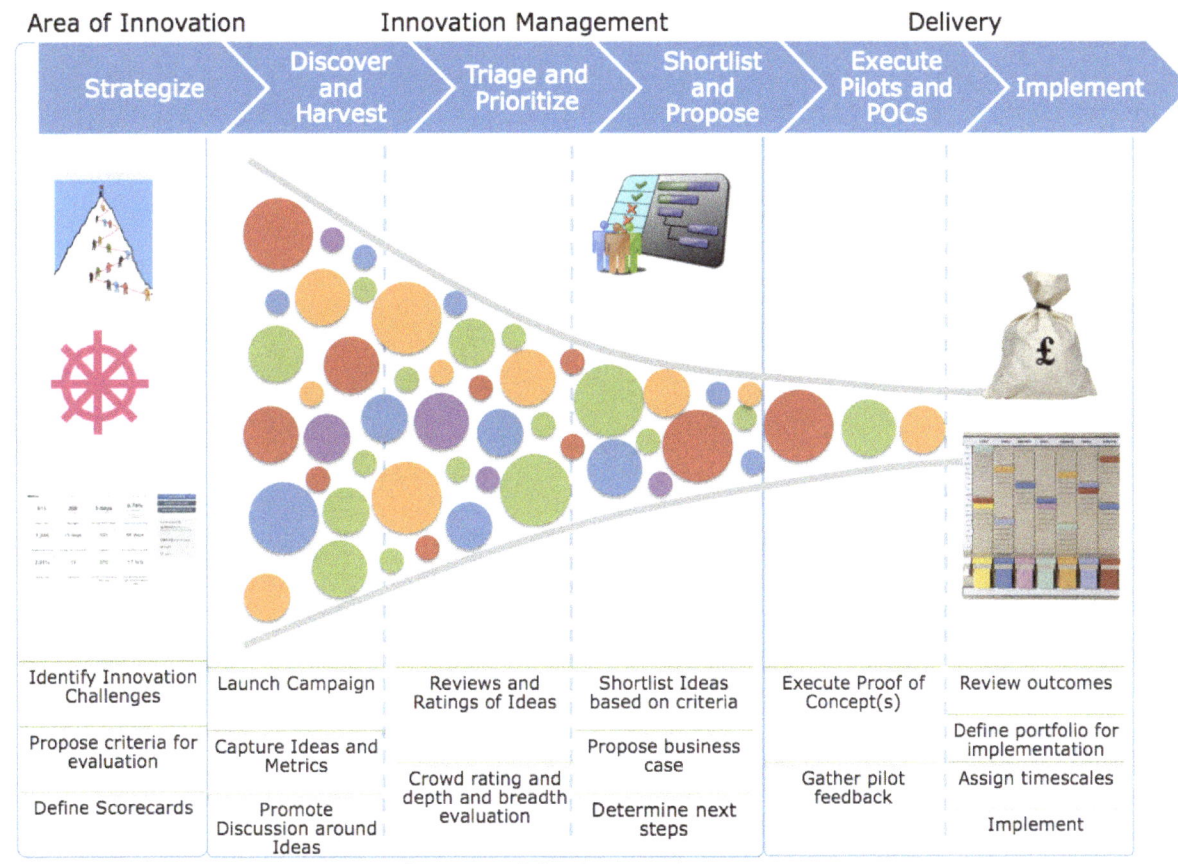

Figure 8: Funnel for innovation management

In its simplest form, the innovation management funnel provides a framework and structure for thinking about the generation and prioritizing of alternative development options, and producing a subset of these into a delivery concept. A variety of different product and process ideas enter the pipeline for investigation, but only a few of these become part of a full-fledged development project.

Managing the innovation management funnel involves three very different tasks. The first is to expand the entrance of the pipeline - the organization must promote its challenges and campaigns in order to increase the number of new product and new process ideas. The second task is to narrow the funnel neck - ideas generated must be prioritized and resources focused on the most attractive opportunities that are aligned with business goals.

The third task is to ensure that the selected projects deliver on the promises and return on investment anticipated when the project was approved.

Kanban provides the enabling mechanism for managing the pipeline. A Kanban board is produced to represent the innovation management funnel.

Stage owners make decisions about reducing the ideas that move through the funnel and stage limits can be used to ensure that ideas move through the funnel.

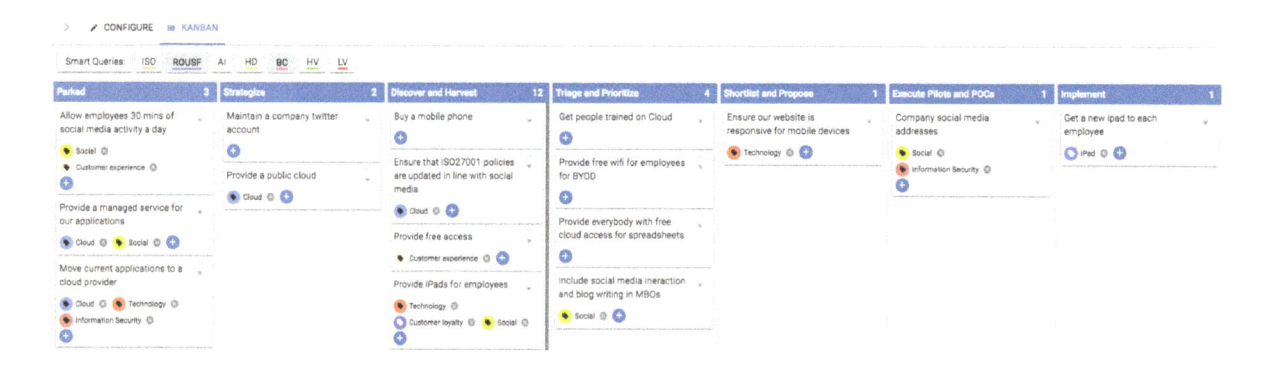

Figure 9: Kanban board

When looking at an innovation management Kanban board, you would expect to see more ideas at the front end stages of the funnel than at the far end where there are fewer ideas implemented.

SOLIDIFYING IDEAS

As ideas move down the funnel and along the Kanban board, the ideas require further detail in order to make decisions about their viability. It may be that some ideas have further attributes that drive these decisions. It may also be the case that ideas drive new requirements and suggested features in products.

Kanban boards can be hierarchical, so ideas can be associated with other concepts of different types that can be managed on other Kanban boards.

Concepts might be on a different stage in a different Kanban board.

In the example in Figure 10, an idea (a) may be in the state having its strategic attributes filled in on the main Kanban board but on an Ideas only Kanban board where the stages are (to do, doing and done), it might still be in the state of 'to do' as our portfolio manager has not reviewed it yet.

Another example is where an idea is being prioritized on the innovation management Kanban that represents our funnel and might link to a requirement (b) that is currently parked, as we don't have anybody to work on it.

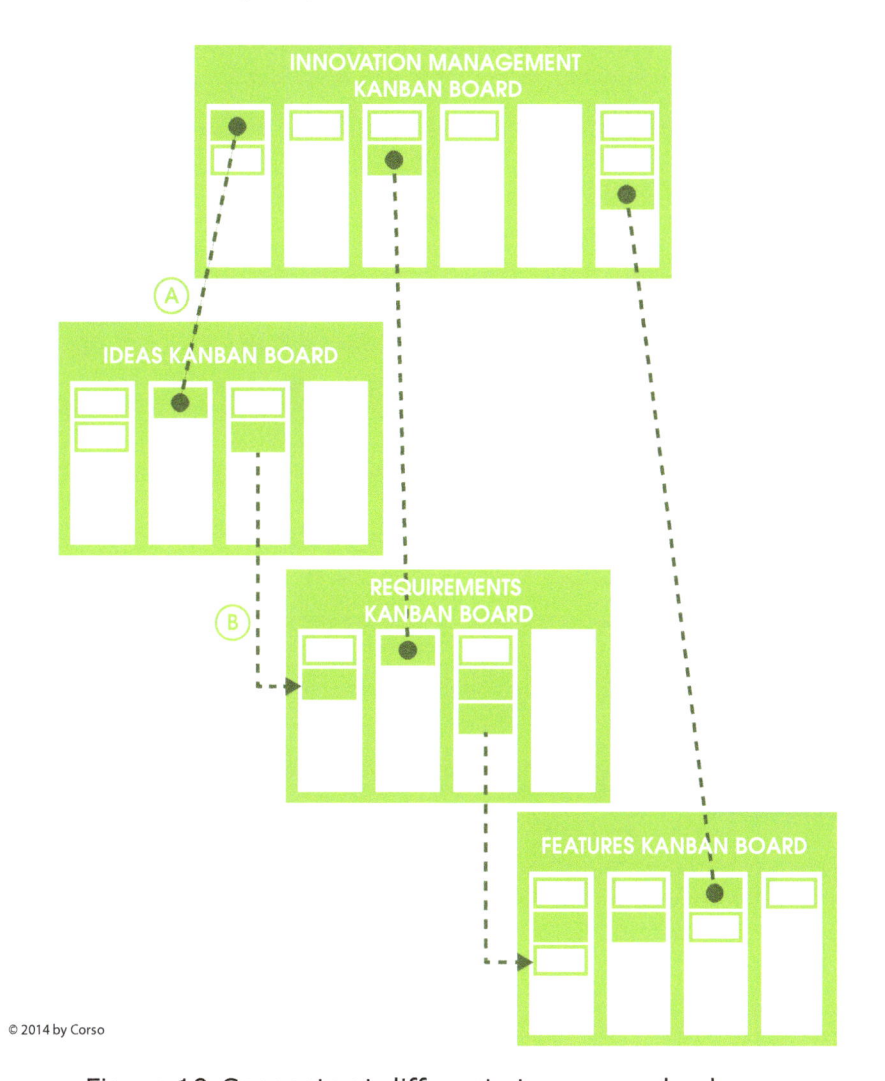

Figure 10: Concepts at different stages on a kanban

Some kanban boards provide rules where concepts can be moved between different stages but not others.

The kanban board may follow work flow rules that may be defined to support a governance structure. For example, signing off the acquisition of an application or project where once approved, it cannot be submitted again.

KANBAN AND ENTERPRISE ARCHITECTURE

When adopting an Agile approach to enterprise architecture, Kanban provide a great way to move work forward at ease to achieve an end goal or objective. Kanban boards provide a "work in progress" view of our enterprise architecture concepts. They provide an ideal way to track the visibility and status of our work in progress and provide a visual set of stages. Each stage contains a set of 'cards' that represent concepts. We've seen many organizations using post-it notes and putting them on walls and white boards to represent cards.

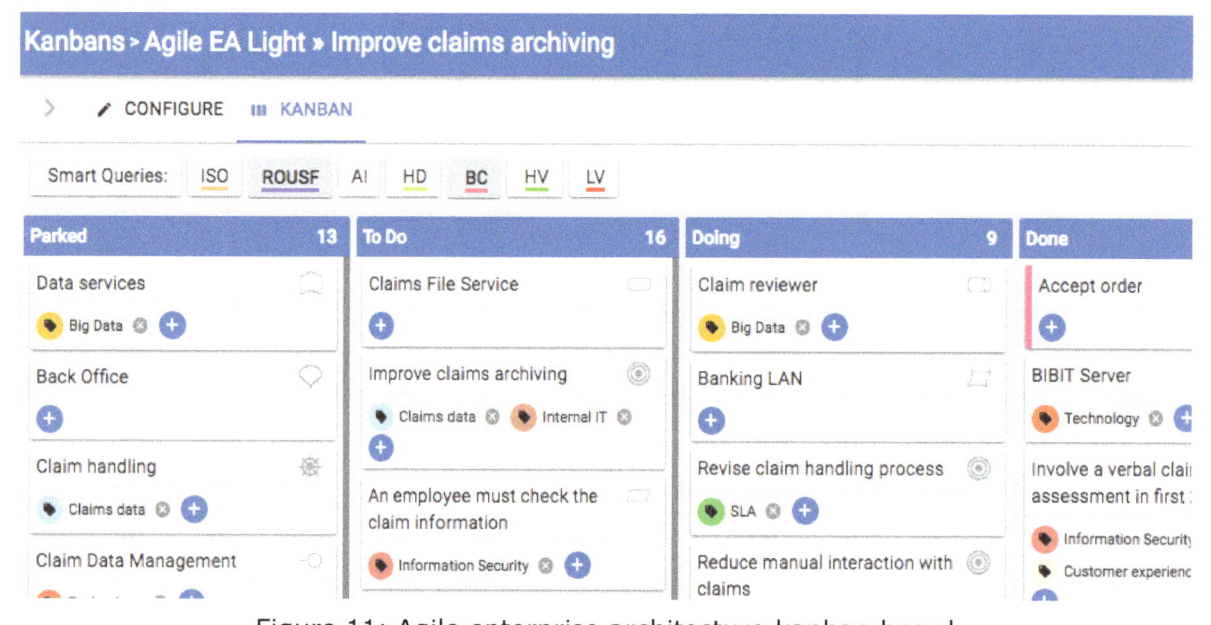

Figure 11: Agile enterprise architecture kanban board

A Kanban board in Agile Enterprise Architecture (EA) could look like Figure 11.

For example, a card could be an idea, business capability or an application component. Each stage is identified by a name and a description of the stage. There are many different ways of defining a Kanban board. A typical board, has the stages – Parked, To Do, Doing and Done. However, most companies tailor the Kanban to suit their own environment and projects.

Kanban boards can also have visual indicators on the concepts (cards) such as colors to indicate status of different attributes.

In the example in Figure 11, we're showing tags as different colors on concepts, where they are tagged or categorized for an organization. This helps identify status of the cards on the kanban and helps decide which we should focus on.

TOGAF ARCHITECTURE DEVELOPMENT METHOD (ADM)

Ideally, work moves from left to right on a Kanban board. We can use the TOGAF Architecture Development Method (ADM) to provide a set of stages for an initial Kanban board displayed in a left to right sequence. The ADM provides an enterprise architecture lifecycle for developing concepts.

Each phase in the ADM that contains concepts and deliverables could be represented as a stage.

Figure 13 shows the TOGAF ADM mapped into a Kanban board.

For each phase in the ADM, we can move concepts around to show where they are in the overall lifecycle to give them overall context. For example, we may be defining a new business capability as part of our Architecture Vision and then move this into our Business Architecture phase for further refinement. In this case, we can put the new business capability into the first stage when we are defining it and move it to the second stage at a later date.

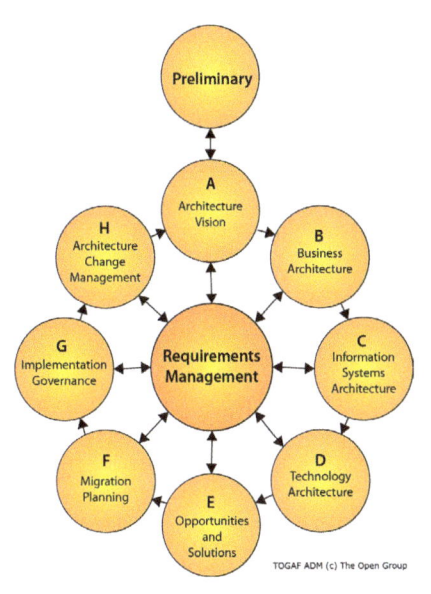

Figure 12: The Open Groups TOGAF ADM

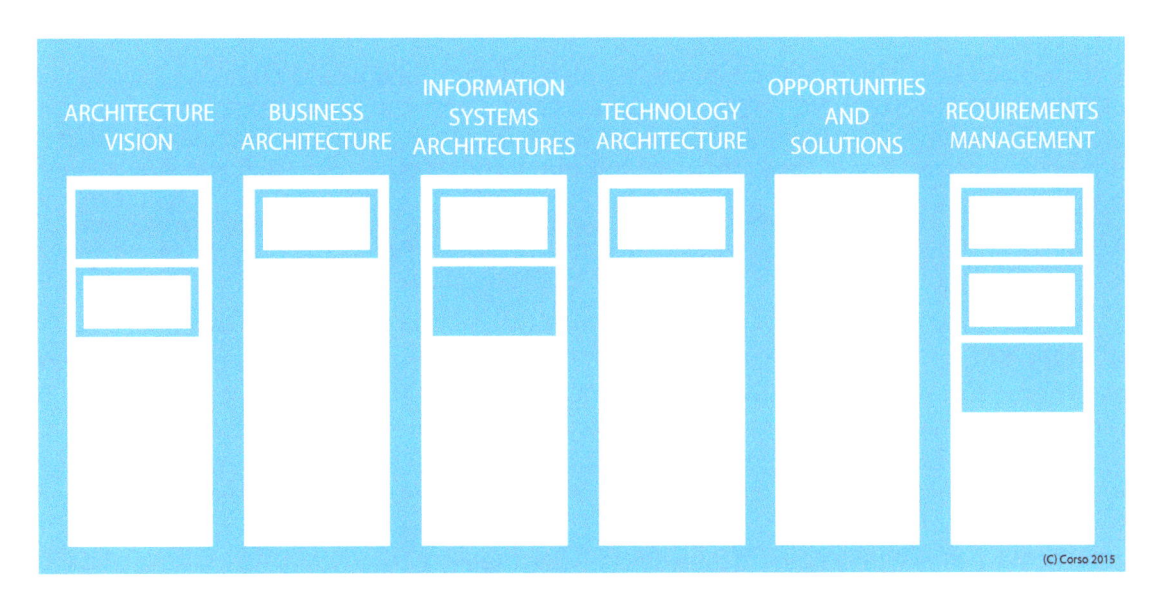

Figure 13: TOGAF ADM kanban board

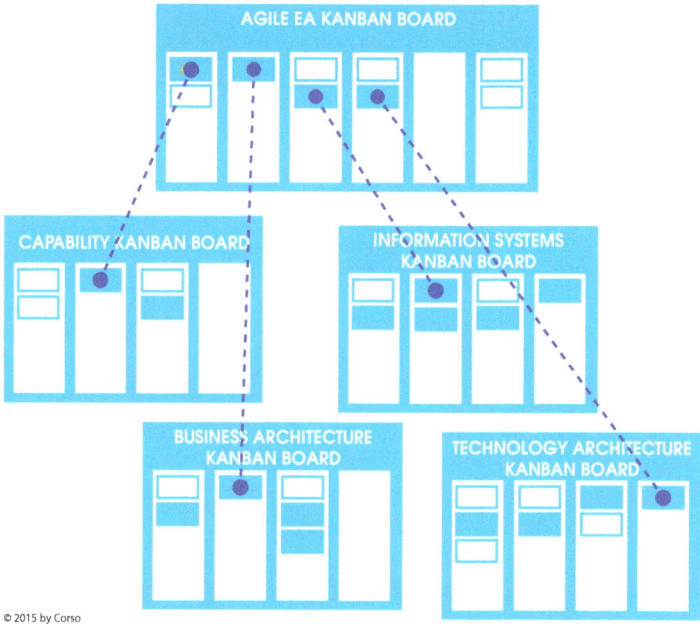

HIERARCHICAL KANBAN BOARDS

We can also make our Kanban boards hierarchical by having different concepts represented on multiple Kanban boards.

Our Agile EA Kanban – TOGAF ADM board is showing the overall phases in the TOGAF ADM. We have individual Kanban boards that show the 'work in progress' for each concept type (meta-type). Typically, these stages are parked in either: To do, Doing and Done.

For example, in Figure 14, we can see the work in progress for an application component is 'done' on the information systems architecture board, and sits in the stage 'information systems architecture' on the Agile EA – TOGAF ADM board.

Figure 14: Hierarchical kanban boards

OWNERS

In order to accurately collaborate with users, owners and collaborators can be assigned to stages and concepts. They are notified automatically when concepts move from one stage to another. Each stage can have a limit as to the number of concepts that can be held on that stage at any particular time, thereby forcing work to be performed and not allowing it to build up over time.

SIBLING KANBAN BOARDS

Where multiple teams are involved in a set of concepts and the work needs to be tracked across different domains or stakeholders, it's often useful to create sibling boards for different communities each with their own specific requirements and language.

In Figure 15, an application component may pass through two sets of stakeholders. Initially, a portfolio manager may assess the application component with financial planning information and suitability for the business. The end result of this exercise is a high value portfolio score

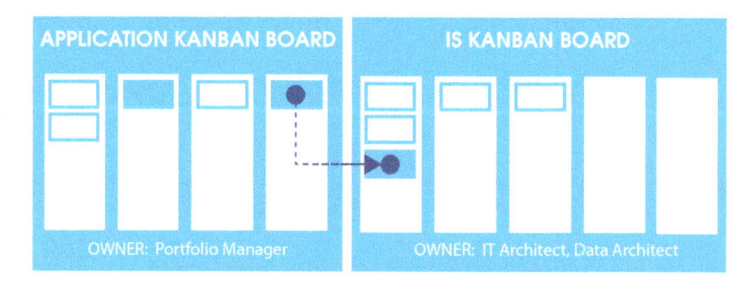

Figure 15: Sibling kanban boards

and the concept is then placed in the 'Done' stage. Following this exercise the IT team may assess the application for IT relevance, risk and complexity with the end result being an IT alignment score. In this case the set of stages for each community are entirely different.

Again, we can see the overall visibility of the concept to see its progress in the work chain and we can force work along the process using stage limits and notifications.

USING KANBAN AS A MECHANISM FOR EA CHANGE

One consistent characteristic of any Enterprise Architecture model is the level of detail it contains and how a particular subset of data can be identified to support any particular change program. In many cases this inability to translate the big picture to a project team undermines the usefulness of the model and casts doubt over the relevance of creating the big picture in the first place.

Having worked with many large Enterprise Architecture models it's always a challenge to find the relevant data for any particular change initiative without creating an additional set of meta-model relationships to manage the process. A good approach is to use tool features to create relevant subsets of data and then walk the subject matter experts (SMEs) through the model so that it's understood, although this often means many hours of building exemplar models but still ends up with the SME taking an involuntary methodology session. In short our SMEs don't always understand Architecture models and don't really need to.

The process of building accurate, relevant models is to involve all parties but in a way that they can effectively collaborate, it needs to be understood that not many stakeholders actually understand architecture but the information that have is vital to the success of building relevant models. It's this knowledge, as architects, that we need to harness but without alienating our sources by presenting complexity.

So how do we create something in context, understandable to a technical but not architecture model savvy audience, that allows us to harvest their knowledge and is relevant to a particular change program?

The answer lies in techniques used in the software development process, particularly agile methods. The issue is managing development tasks within a small team but embracing the wider stakeholder group but delivering just enough to meet requirements. This approach is Kanban, and by borrowing the technique albeit with a more abstract usage, we have created something that is proving successful in creating the contextual models that are needed during the change process.

KANBAN AND AGILITY

Kanban derives from the just in time manufacturing methods that revolutionized manufacturing by focusing on what is needed to achieve a particular result and integrating the supply chain to maximize production. In the Agile EA approach the production line is our contextual architecture for a particular change program or project and our supply chain in the myriad group of SMEs, Partners, Suppliers and the overall Enterprise Architecture model. It's by connecting these parts that we can produce accurate, relevant, verified models to support the project teams that will implement the changes within the organization.

The agile EA approach places Kanban at the heart of managing the change context model and provides a clear focus on which elements of the architecture are needed in a particular context and provides direct connection to the wider stakeholders for collaboration.

So for a practical example let's look at a particular change. In this case it's an insurance company that wishes to approve concepts that affect our application portfolio. As an architect I will make some assumptions about what is involved, I can use the model to understand core associations and context, which provides me with a set of concepts that will most likely be relevant. I place these on a Kanban board.

A Kanban board will have a number of stages that all the relevant concepts will pass through, some may be deemed to be out of scope, and that will be recorded too. The stages represent the process that is to be followed for approval of various assets in the architecture and the concepts on the board represent the context for our change/approval.

Figure 16: Approval lifecycle kanban for application portfolio management

Generically, kanban board stages are flexible and can accommodate any process including formal approaches such as the TOGAF ADM and subsets such as application portfolio management. Figure 17 shows the same concepts but within an application portfolio

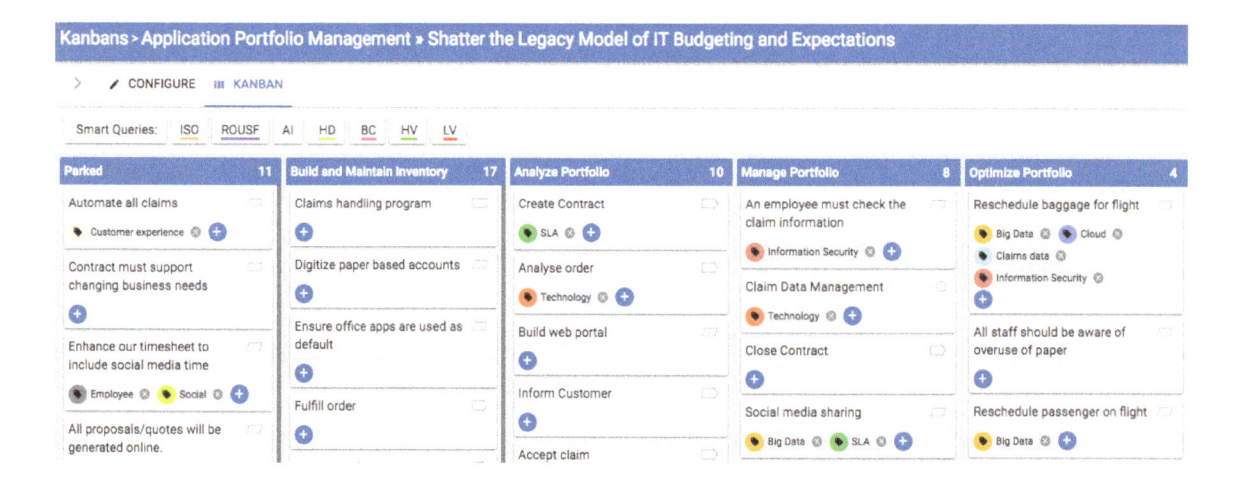

Figure 17: APM concepts on an APM specific kanban board

management process. The same concepts are represented in different stages within a different Kanban, the same concept is likely to apply to other change programs and so likely be represented in different Kanban views and in different stages. In this case it is very easy to understand where a similar concept is involved in different change projects providing a cross project view, this is a key to realizing dependencies and can be a significant analysis tool when deciding the order of delivering different projects.

The core use of this Kanban is for collaboration; each of the concepts can be shared with other members of the team and the wider group of SME's or partners as necessary to fully understand each concept. For example a particular Application Component can be shared with the System owner who can view that particular page and validate assumptions or feedback any necessary changes that are required, this could be discovery of additional interfaces, incorrect values against particular attributes, updated financial or ownership data.

Importantly the SME doesn't need to understand how to model as all the properties and associations are available via a single page in simple tabular form. The SME just makes comments and the architecture team amends or adds new information to the Kanban as required. The model is updated, has been validated and the owner of the actual component has been directly involved in the process. We simply move the concept to the next stage of the Kanban and continue with the other concepts until finally we can conclude the modeling exercise. The completeness of the Kanban can be visualized by looking at how many concepts have move into either a goal stage or have been parked (rejected). The validated contextual model can then be migrated back into the overall model for other change projects to use in a similar manner.

This approach, borrowed from the agile development world, provides a simple, intuitive way of working with just enough architecture to deliver a model to achieve a single goal. Along the way we have engaged with our SMEs to ensure that the model is capable of providing the basis for change, made the EA model a key part of the solution and ensured that our overall model is maintained in a state that can be used by other project teams, SME's and partners with a confidence that seldom occurs within an Enterprise Architecture modeling environment.

TASKS

Tasks and Kanban boards are intertwined. Kanban boards drive our ability to manage tasks. However, as individuals, it's important to understand time management when it comes to our productivity. With only a set window of time each day to accomplish what we need to, it makes sense to use this time as wisely as possible.

If we want to be truly productive it is not our time that we should be managing so closely, it is our tasks. When we manage our tasks well, we automatically manage our time well too.

Here are some tips to help you achieve better task and time management as a result.

PRIORITIZE YOUR TASKS

Identify what tasks will make the most difference to your project and prioritize them accordingly.

Your first priority should always be the work that will have consequences if you don't finish it today, closely followed by work that will generate you short-term income. Once these tasks are completed, you then move on to the ordinary everyday tasks that keep your business running as usual and the business development tasks that will help you continue your business growth.

You should use a task manager and if possible an integrated task manager with your enterprise architecture and innovation management platform.

PUT A TIME LIMIT AND DEADLINE ON EACH TASK

We put a timeline on goals, so why not on tasks too? Every task on your to-do list should have a due date and the maximum time limit you want to spend on it that day. This is particularly important for open ended tasks like e-mail, social media management and follow up that have the potential to drain more of your time and take you away from other important tasks you need to complete.

UPGRADE YOUR PRODUCTIVITY, EVALUATE YOUR TASKS REGULARLY

Before each of your work breaks quickly evaluate your task list and progress. Check your task manager in the morning before you begin work.

Do you need to make any changes to your list now based on new information like a new concept or change of deadline? Are the tasks you're doing and yet to do really a priority?

Based on your evaluation, delegate or outsource tasks that are not a profitable or productive use of your time and rearrange your list to reflect your new priorities. Invite other stakeholders to contribute if it helps you complete tasks quickly. Continue to keep yourself accountable to ensure your time is going towards the most important tasks.

TASKS, INNOVATION MANAGEMENT AND ENTERPRISE ARCHITECTURE

Tasks should be created for specific concepts in your model and are usually tied to a concept. This ensures that the collaboration is always for a concept on the platform or a function you are doing such as comparing using pairwise comparisons.

Ensure that you document tasks with any useful links. For example, it might be useful to link a task with a set of company documents that already exist.

Attachments can also be uploaded for a task. The benefit here being that tasks can be augmented with further documentation, for example a presentation explaining some thinking around an idea.

If you're inviting others to collaborate around your task, specify a Role for them. This is useful in informing the collaborators within a task, what the role of the individuals is in the task. For example, we may want an 'expert' to provide their opinion on the task and therefore could write Expert in the Role attribute.

If you're using an automated task management environment, a collaborator is usually informed by e-mail that they have been assigned to a task. A collaborator should also see the task in their own personal task list with their role. Tasks have a strong affiliation with Work Packages. Work Packages are described in detail in a later chapter. Any task that is being worked on cannot only belong to a Kanban but may also be part of a work package that is being undertaken. This can be modelled as part of your architecture.

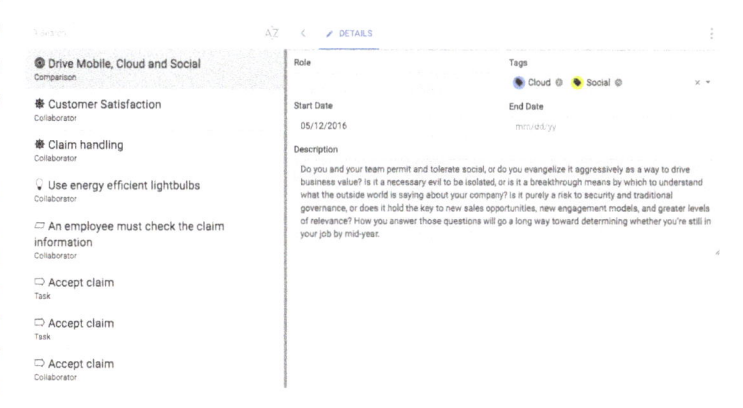

Figure 18: Example task manager

COLLABORATION SUMMARY

Although Kanban boards can be created using post it notes and whiteboards, electronic Kanban boards are now much more popular.

Kanban boards are an ideal way to manage work in progress and to track these within a method such as TOGAF®. Without such a mechanism, it's extremely difficult to be agile. A Kanban board should be created with a goal in mind and the stages, concepts, owners and limits should reflect the goal that is being sought. The Kanban provides a daily progress input into agile approaches such as scrum and/or daily stand up meetings. Tasks are for individuals to manage their workload and priorities.

CHAPTER 8

GAMIFICATION

INTRODUCTION

In this chapter we touch on gamification and why gamification is important to both enterprise architecture (EA) and innovation management (IM). The section provides the theory behind gamification and some examples of its usage within enterprise planning.

OVERVIEW

Gamification brings elements of traditional game play to drive engagement and behavior. Traditionally, engagement of stakeholders has been critical to the success of innovation and enterprise architecture initiatives.

Game players typically exhibit persistence, risk taking, attention to detail and problem solving. All behaviors that would ideally be suited to management of EA and IM.

Many EA projects fail through disengagement of the wider community. IM can suffer from a lack of persistence in taking a qualified idea through to delivery of that idea.

Gamification can help by providing mechanisms to engage and retain communities through these endeavours.

DETAIL AND TECHNIQUES

There are really 4 objectives that we're looking to address with gamification:

1. Fostering engagement
2. Inspiring loyalty
3. Increasing conversions
4. Building a community

The objectives help us to make our innovation management and enterprise architecture practices a success.

FOSTERING ENGAGEMENT

We want to engage as many stakeholders as possible and we want them to add value to our programs. We can encourage various behaviors whereby stakeholders want to return and contribute. We can also provide key performance indicators that demonstrate the success of our engagement strategy.

Examples of behaviours that foster engagement

Behavior	KPI
Posting a comment	Number of comments
Writing a blog post	Number of blog posts
Reading existing content	Number of page views
Voting on content	Number of votes
Rating content	Number of ratings entered

INSPIRING LOYALTY

When we want to encourage users to use a feature, we can encourage various behaviors to inspire them to use the platform more often. We can also inspire loyalty around themes such as innovation management campaigns.

Examples of behaviours that inspire loyalty

Behavior	KPI
Acquiring more users	Number of new users
Logging in	Number of Login's
Viewing a page	Number of page views

INCREASING CONVERSIONS

The big problem with conversions is the catch-22 situation of attracting stakeholders and converting them to reviewers of your EA and IM content. Without collaboration you can't attract users, and without users you don't get collaboration. So how do you get people to collaborate time and again?

Examples of behaviours that increase conversions

Behavior	KPI
Exploring various different EA and IM views	Number of page views of EA and IM views
Visiting other users' content	Number of page views of other users' content
Reading comments of the content	Number of page views of comments

BUILDING COMMUNITIES

Innovation management and agile enterprise architecture requires the input of a community of stakeholders. But how do you build a community and how does gamification help?

The following behaviors all help build a community.

Examples of behaviours that build communities

Behavior	KPI
Leaving comments	Number of comments
Writing reviews	Number of reviews
Giving a 'thumbs up' or 'high five'	Number of 'thumbs up' or 'high fives'
Asking a question	Number of questions asked
Answering a question	Number of questions answered
Sharing an idea	Number of ideas shared

MISSIONS AND CHALLENGES

Missions and challenges are synonyms in gamification. They require users to perform a prescribed set of game play actions, following a defined route. A mission might involve a single step (for example, entering an idea) or several steps.

Often, the steps in a mission must occur in a certain sequence. These missions are called progression missions. Other times, actions can occur in any sequence. These are called random missions.

The tasks in a mission might revolve around the same game play behavior (reading five posts, for example), or could involve different game play behaviors (for example, viewing a diagram, commenting on a diagram, adding a concept to a diagram and adding your own diagram).

When these techniques are used within a platform, an organization can design their own missions and objectives that satisfy their particular business goals (for example, a mission to ensure that stakeholders respond to a campaign in innovation management).

Gamification can be visualized in a number of ways. These include leader boards, badges and enhanced profiles for users within a community.

BADGE THEMES

There are various elements of gaming that we can harness for enterprise architecture and innovation management purposes.

Some example badges and rewards follow:

Cascading information: Unlock information continuously		**Investment**: Feel pride in your work in the program	
⭐	**Bonuses** - receive unexpected rewards	👍	**Achievements** - earn public recognition for completing work
⏱	**Countdown** - tackle challenges in a fixed amount of time	📅	**Appointments** - check in to receive new challenges
🔍	**Discovery** - navigate through learning and unpick areas of knowledge	👥	**Collaboration** - work with others to achieve goals
🛟	**Loss aversion** - play to avoid losing what you have gained	🏆	**Epic meaning** - work to achieve something sublime or transcendent
🎮	**Infinite play** - play continuously until you become an expert	👤	**Virality** - be incentivized to involve others
🔧	**Synthesis** - work on challenges that require multiple skills to solve		

Progression: Success can be visualized incrementally			
🔒	**Levels** - ramp up and unlock content	🛡	**Points** - increase the running numerical value of your work

Thus we can see that many of the elements in gamification can be tied directly to some of the pain points that are experienced in enterprise architecture and innovation programs.

SUMMARY

Although, it may seem like gamification requires you to have an interactive way for your stakeholders to participate, there are more convenient ways you can use this strategy and apply it to your innovation management and enterprise architecture as a very powerful tool.   Many organizations might use this in a manner such as having online tooling that offers badges and points, but even without tooling you can also benefit from this in different ways. Make sure you always have your campaigns or architecture KPIs updated and share them on social media. Most companies opt for sharing this on internal social media platforms such as Yammer or SharePoint and using gamification on other social media platforms as well.

Remember that you don't have to use gamification, it depends on your organizations' culture.

CHAPTER 9

MODELS AND VIEWS

INTRODUCTION

This chapter explains the concept of models and views. Models and views underpin any enterprise architecture and innovation management platform and capability. Unlike spreadsheets and presentation tools, having a consistent underlying model with views allows an organization to have an authentic representation of its information.

A model and views are fundamental to managing and communicating enterprise architecture.

OVERVIEW

A model represents the data for an organization that describes the enterprise architecture and innovation management concepts. It is based upon the underlying meta-model provided by an enterprise architecture framework.

Most frameworks include a default set of views. The ArchiMate® specification from the Open Group provides a set of views along with their underlying notation so that you can recognize a concept from its visualization.

A view is a work product that can be used to communicate, analyze and manage enterprise architecture models. A view is also a representation of a model from the perspective of a viewpoint.

This viewpoint on a model focuses on specific concerns regarding the model that suppresses details to provide a simplified model.

For example, a financial portfolio viewpoint focuses on financial portfolio concerns and a financial portfolio viewpoint model contains those elements that are related to financial concerns from a more general model.

Views allow you to manage the abstraction of a model so that it is relevant to different stakeholders.

A business stakeholder may have a high level goal oriented viewpoint and a software developer may have a detailed technical viewpoint of a model.

VIEWS

Views are represented in different ways according to stakeholder needs.

In this chapter, we are focusing on diagrams, which are a common way for most enterprise architecture frameworks to represent views.

However, later chapters also cover other types of views such as pivot tables, charts, Kanban boards and roadmaps that are all different perspectives on the underlying model.

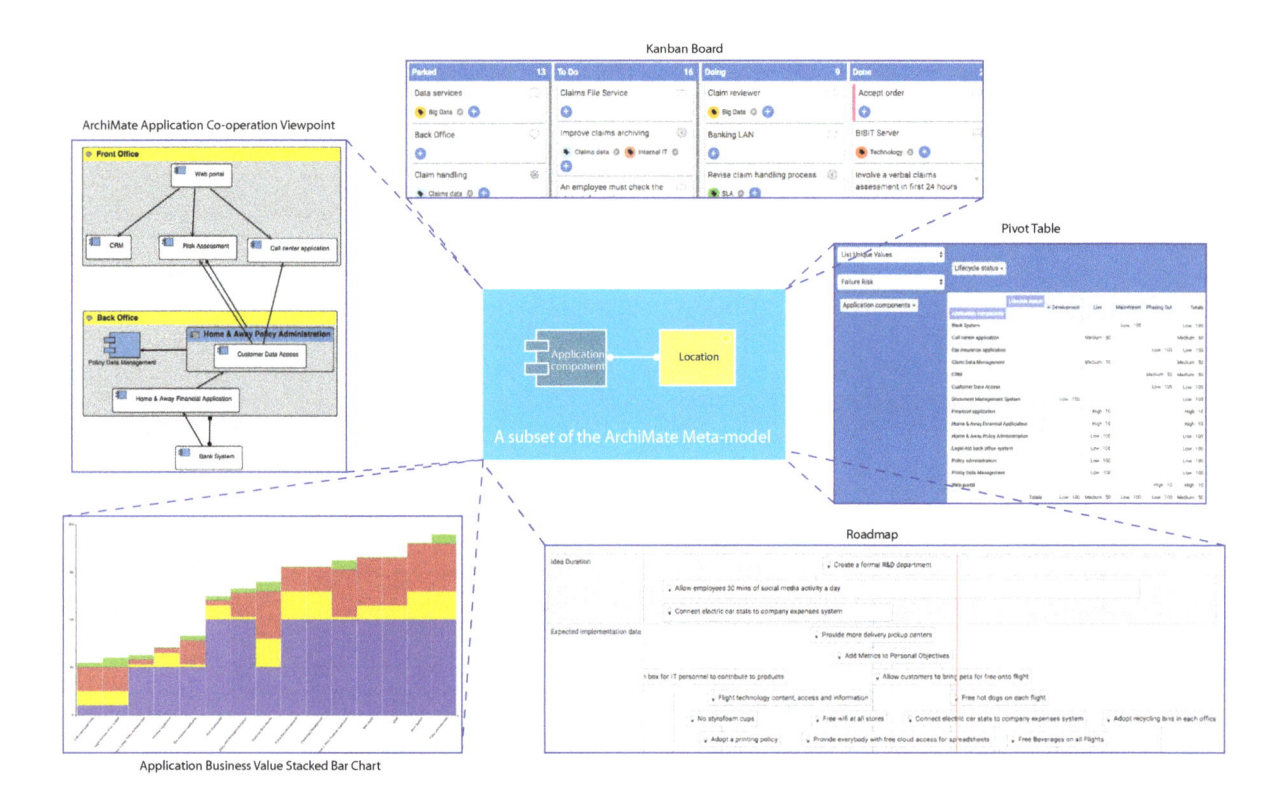

Figure 19: Multiple views for a single model

Figure 19 shows some sample views of a subset of the meta-model. Here we are showing application components and assignments to locations.

You can see that there are many different views of the architecture depending on stakeholders needs.

DIAGRAMS

Diagrams provide a view of the underlying repository concepts and their associations.

The Open Group ArchiMate® 2.1 specification contains a core set of views, an implementation and migration extension and motivation views.

These are the example views provided by the Open Group. However, ArchiMate® is not limited to just this collection of views. You may also create your own views (meta-diagrams) to suit your own purposes.

The Corso Agile EA package also adds Business Capability extensions, so we've included these views in the appendix at the back of this book.

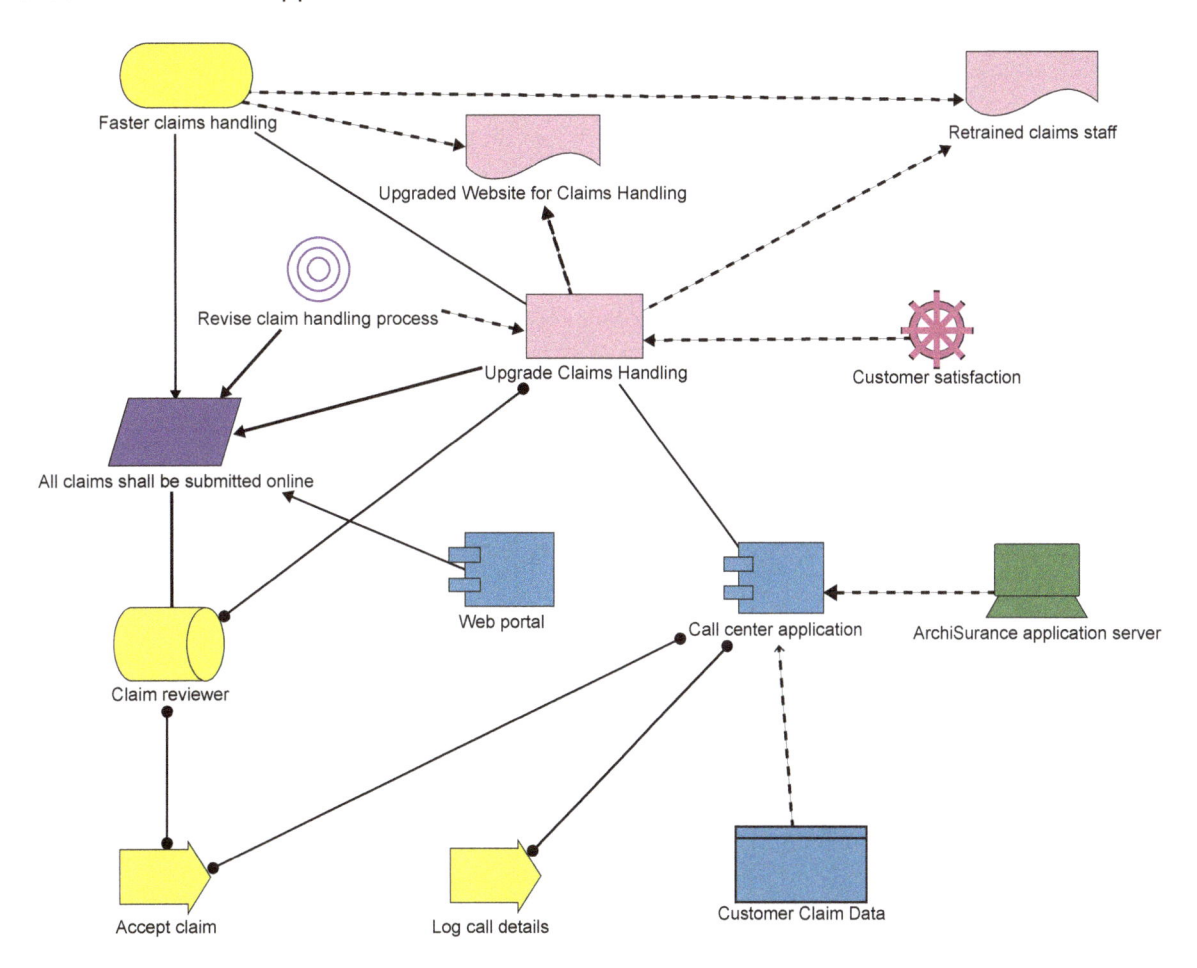

Figure 20: Example layered view

Figure 20 is an example 'layered' view from ArchiMate®. The layered view is useful as it contains nearly all of the meta-types and meta-associations in the ArchiMate® meta-model.

You can see on this view that we are focusing in the centre on the 'Upgrade Claims Handling' work package. We're also showing the connected associations that this work package has to other concepts.

The other concepts include the driver: 'Customer satisfaction', goal: Revise claim handling process, application component: Call centre application, deliverable: Upgraded Website for Claims Handling, requirement: All claims shall be submitted online, business service: Faster claims handling and role: Claim reviewer. Each of these associations is different and is represented in a different graphical manner.

The layered view is also useful for showing the layers between the different domains of the architecture. In Figure 21, the layers are depicted with different colors. Yellow icons represent the business layer, blue icons for the application layer and green icons for the technology layer.

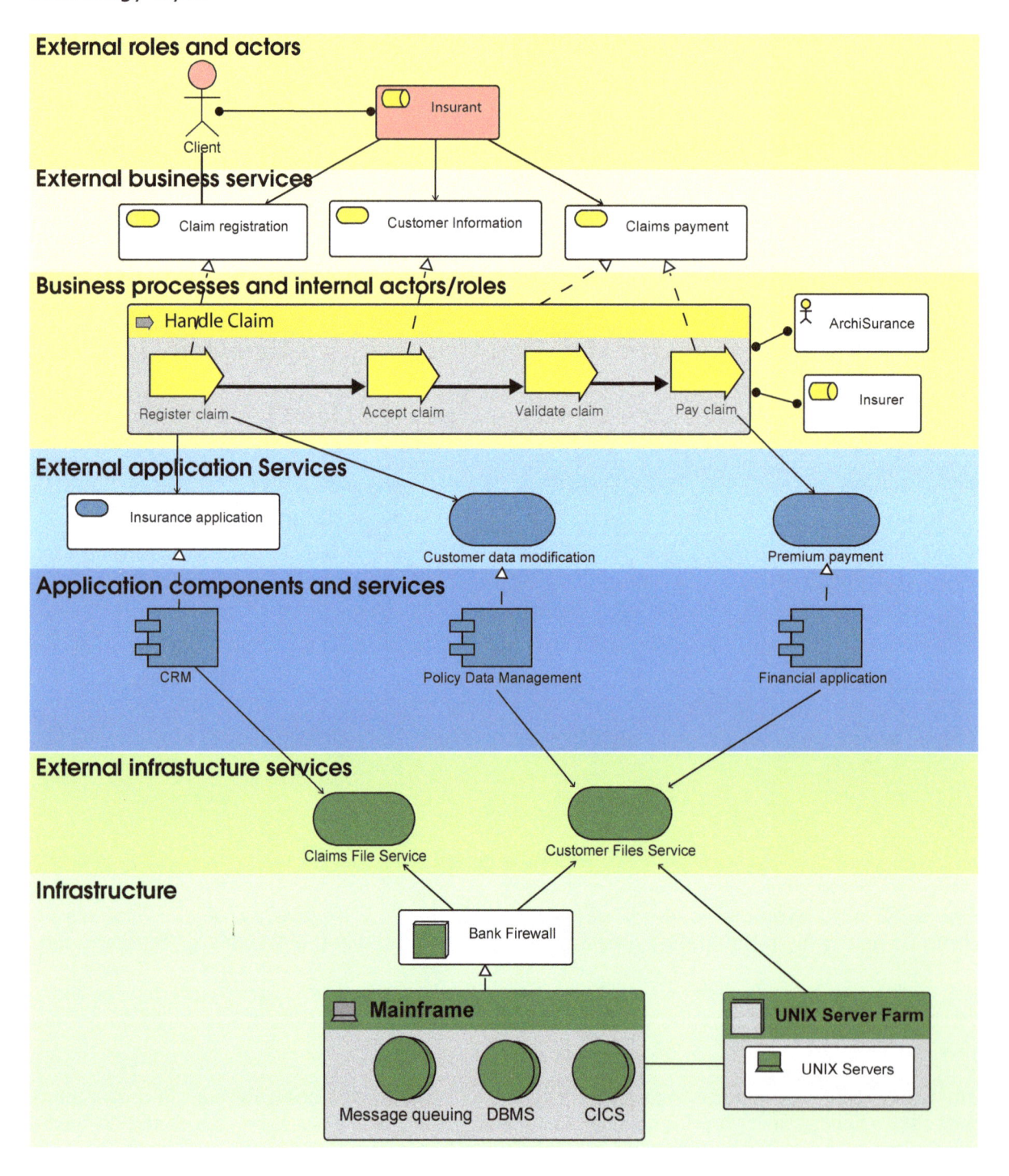

Figure 21: ArchiMate layered view showing layers

REPRESENTATIONAL CONSISTENCY

Many of these viewpoints can be created by hand or in drawing tool, however, a major benefit of having a model and ideally a repository-based tool is that your views are consistent. That is, they are represented directly based upon the associations in the repository.

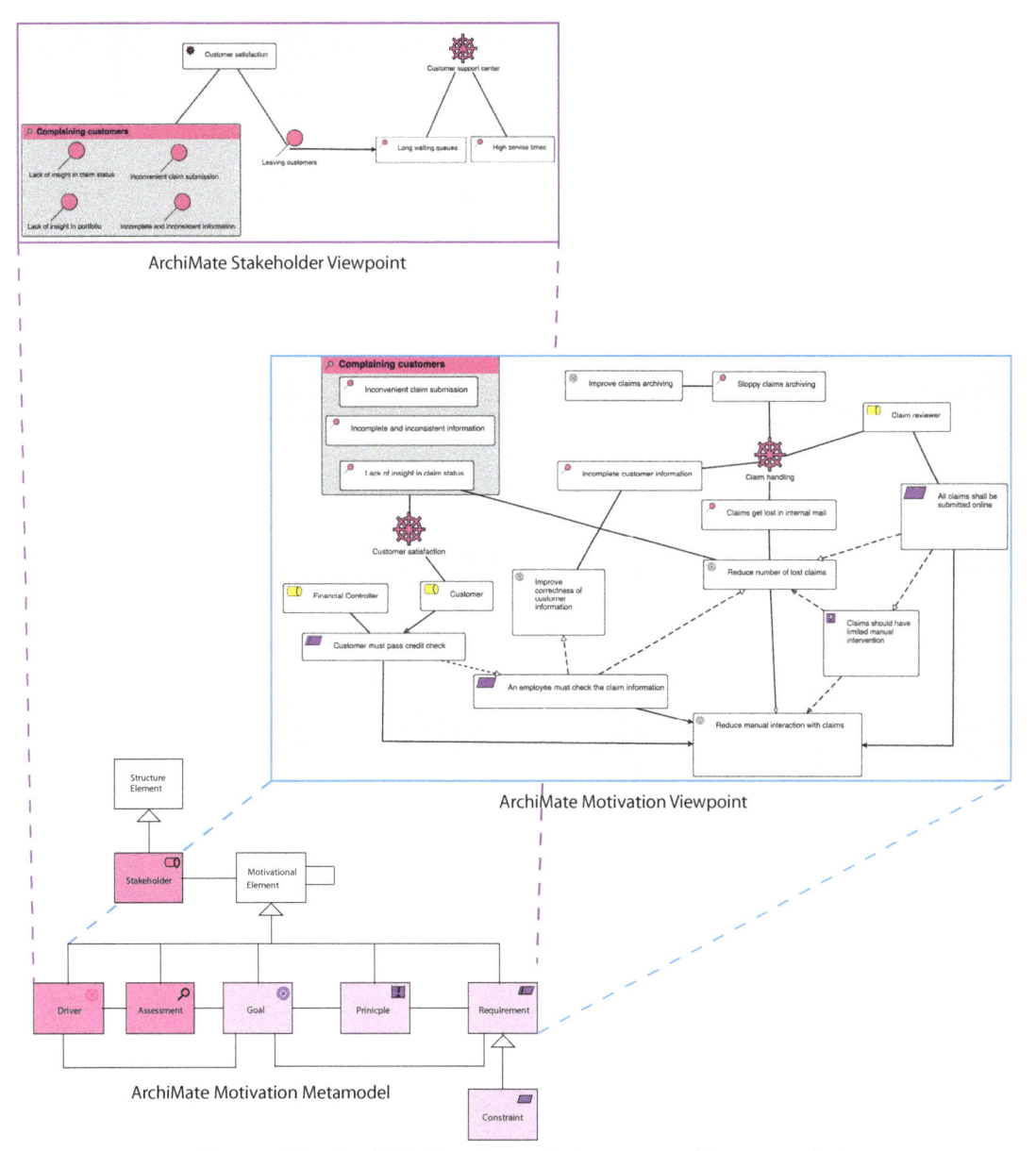

Figure 22: ArchiMate viewpoints mapped to a model

No matter what type of view, the information should always be representationally consistent with the model.

However, for the sake of visibility, it is a good idea to sometimes hide associations and detail in views to match stakeholder needs.

In Figure 22, we can see that we have two very different viewpoints for the same underlying meta-model.

The ArchiMate® Stakeholder Viewpoint shows the drivers and assessments. You can see that some of the same concepts are represented in the ArchiMate® Motivation Viewpoint which is showing the overall motivational strategy for our business.

All associations that are shown exist in the repository. When a diagram is created, you should expect your tool to show the associations that exist between two concepts automatically.

CUSTOM VIEWPOINTS

Architecture frameworks such as ArchiMate® and TOGAF® provide a set of views. In the case of ArchiMate®, the views are example views and ones which a user of the framework may find useful.

Most of the enterprise architecture frameworks are designed to support custom views. That is, a set of views that helps a stakeholder comprehend the architecture.

A few example custom views that we've found useful are in the reference guide at the back of this book.

We do recommend though that you discuss what views are required by your stakeholders to communicate and represent their needs and build them accordingly. You'll then be encouraging them to be part of the innovation and enterprise architecture practice.

SUMMARY

Views provide a representational consistent view of the underlying model. Views can contain as much detail or as little detail necessary to communicate the model to the appropriate stakeholder.

Diagrams are the most popular form of views and ArchiMate® provides a standard notation for the communication of views. The benefit of this being that each stakeholder has the same understanding of any concept. This is much like any builder will be able to understand any set of building plans no matter who the author as they use the same design standards.

For a full list of diagram views, please see the ArchiMate® reference guide in the Appendix to this book.

CHAPTER 10

ROADMAPPING

INTRODUCTION

This chapter explains the concept of roadmapping and how it relates to enterprise architecture and innovation management

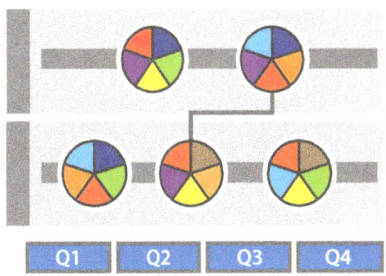

OVERVIEW

The focus of innovation and Agile EA is on increasing the agility of the business. This means it is essential that an organization understands where it will be at any given period of time.

As 'time to market' and the ability to change quickly are vital for organizations to keep pace and innovate then roadmaps are a critical view on how complex or what the impact of change is.

ENTERPRISE ARCHITECTURE ROADMAPS

The enterprise architecture concepts provide a blueprint of the organization. Many aspects of these concepts can be described with a time dimension. The time dimension can be used to either display a milestone date at which something is expected to happen, or a date range within which something will take place.

INNOVATION MANAGEMENT ROADMAPS

Innovation management is a framework for responding to ideas and implementing those ideas to keep ahead of the game. Business change is motivated by time and speed to market. Adding a 'temporal' dimension to innovation allows you to respond and view the innovation concepts over a period of time.

ROADMAP VIEWS

Just like a diagram is a view of an architecture model, so is a roadmap.

Roadmaps are views on the enterprise architecture and innovation management concepts from a time perspective. A roadmap is usually defined as a view for a specific time period. E.g. 1 year or the next 3 months.

Roadmaps may be dynamic and reflect the state of the concept at any moment in time in real-time, or they may be static and show how a set of concepts looked at any moment in time.

Many concepts can have multiple time attributes that represent different time properties.

In enterprise architecture, an application component may have a set of lifecycle times that are associated with it such as 'live' or 'sunset'.

Another innovation management example is that an idea may have an anticipated implementation date, representing when this idea is expected to be implemented in order for it to be of business value. An Idea may also have a duration for when the idea is valid if an idea needs time boxing. For example, an idea might be to take advantage of a government subsidy. The subsidy is only available for 3 months from Jan 2017-Mar 2017.

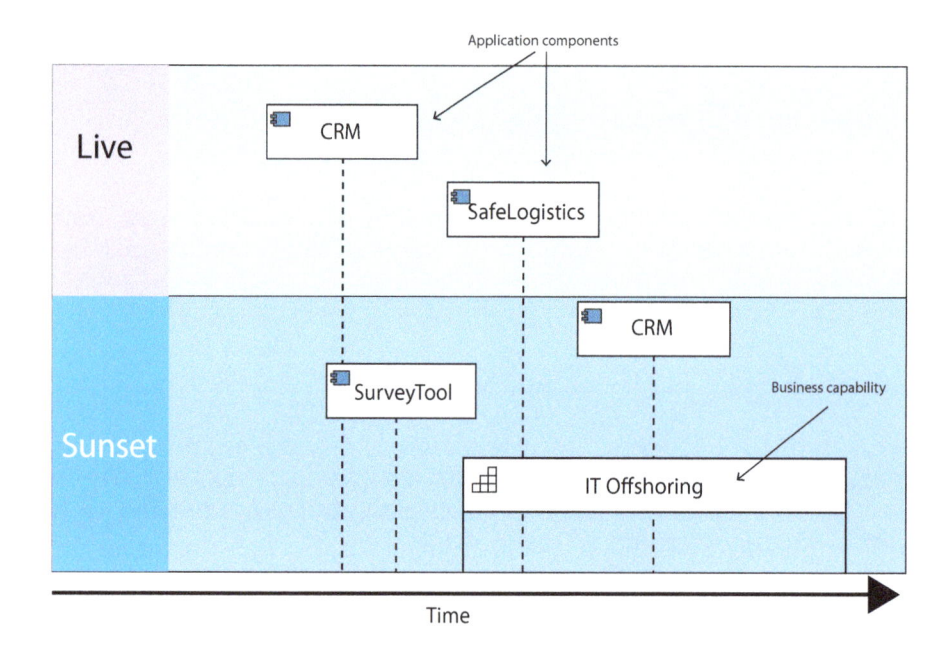

Figure 23: A simple roadmap

Time attributes may simply be a single date such as a milestone or be a time period between two dates.

A roadmap view can consist of lanes. The lanes will show any theme or category for a set of concepts. A roadmap may be divided up to show different types of concepts on one roadmap.

For example, it may be useful to show work package duration and the anticipated Idea implementation dates so we can see if our plans are on track.

Time usually flows from left to right on a roadmap diagram.

Figure 23 is an example showing different time properties for application components:

As we can see in Figure 23, we have two lanes, live and sunset. These are themes that we may well be interested in.

We are showing on a single roadmap view both application components (CRM, SafeLogistics, SurveyTool) and a business capability (IT Offshoring).

We can show application components with the live date attribute in the live lane.

We can also view the business capability but with a sunset time period. The time period is between two dates. We can display the application component sunset milestone dates in this sunset lane too.

In this example, it takes a much longer time to phase out a business capability and we only want to show the single milestone period for our applications.

This view gives us a good visibility of concepts with differing time dimensions.

We can also see for a single application component, it's live and sunset dates in different lanes, so we can compare.

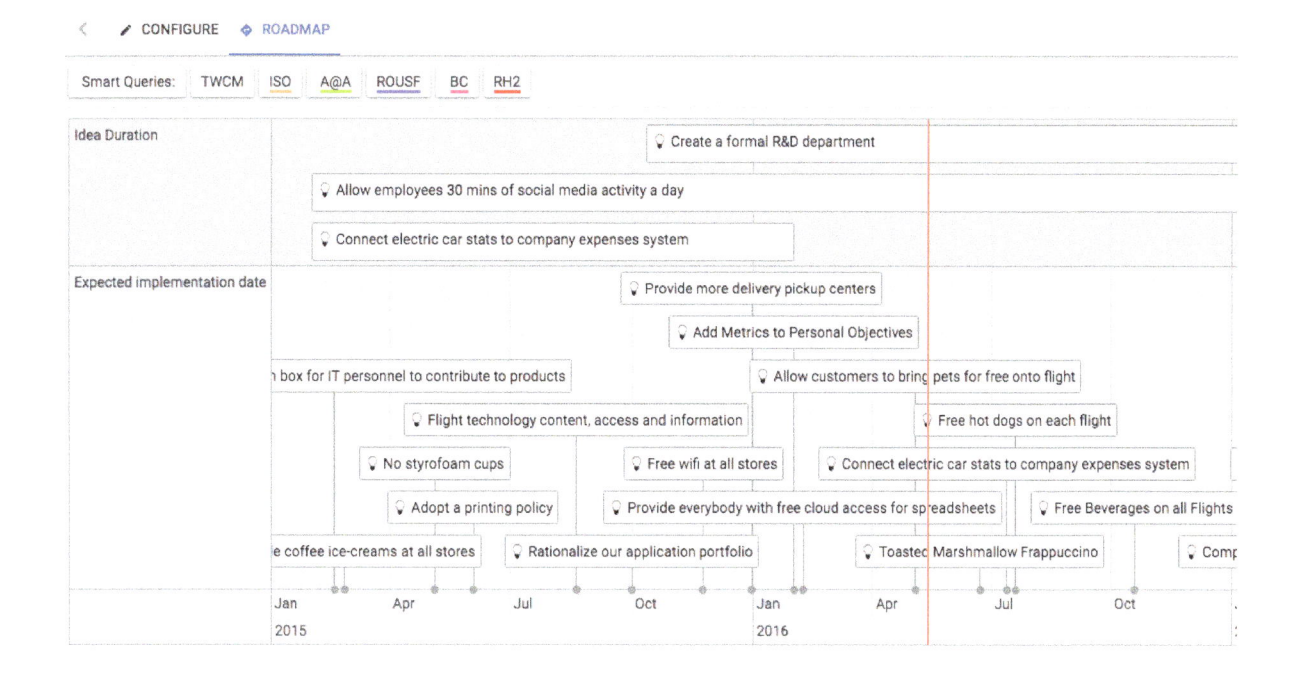

Figure 24: Innovation management roadmap

Innovation Management Example

Figure 24 is an example showing different date attributes for ideas:

As you can, we have two lanes, Expected Implementation Date and Ideas Duration. These are themes that we may well be interested in.

We are showing on a single roadmap view both time attributes (Expected Implementation Date and Ideas Duration) and you can see that come concepts will be represented in both lanes.

You can see that for some idea, we are expecting the idea to be implemented within a time frame (duration). You can also see the implementation date for concepts within that time frame.

Note that a single vertical line represents a single date with a circle on the date line and a time span stretches two dates.

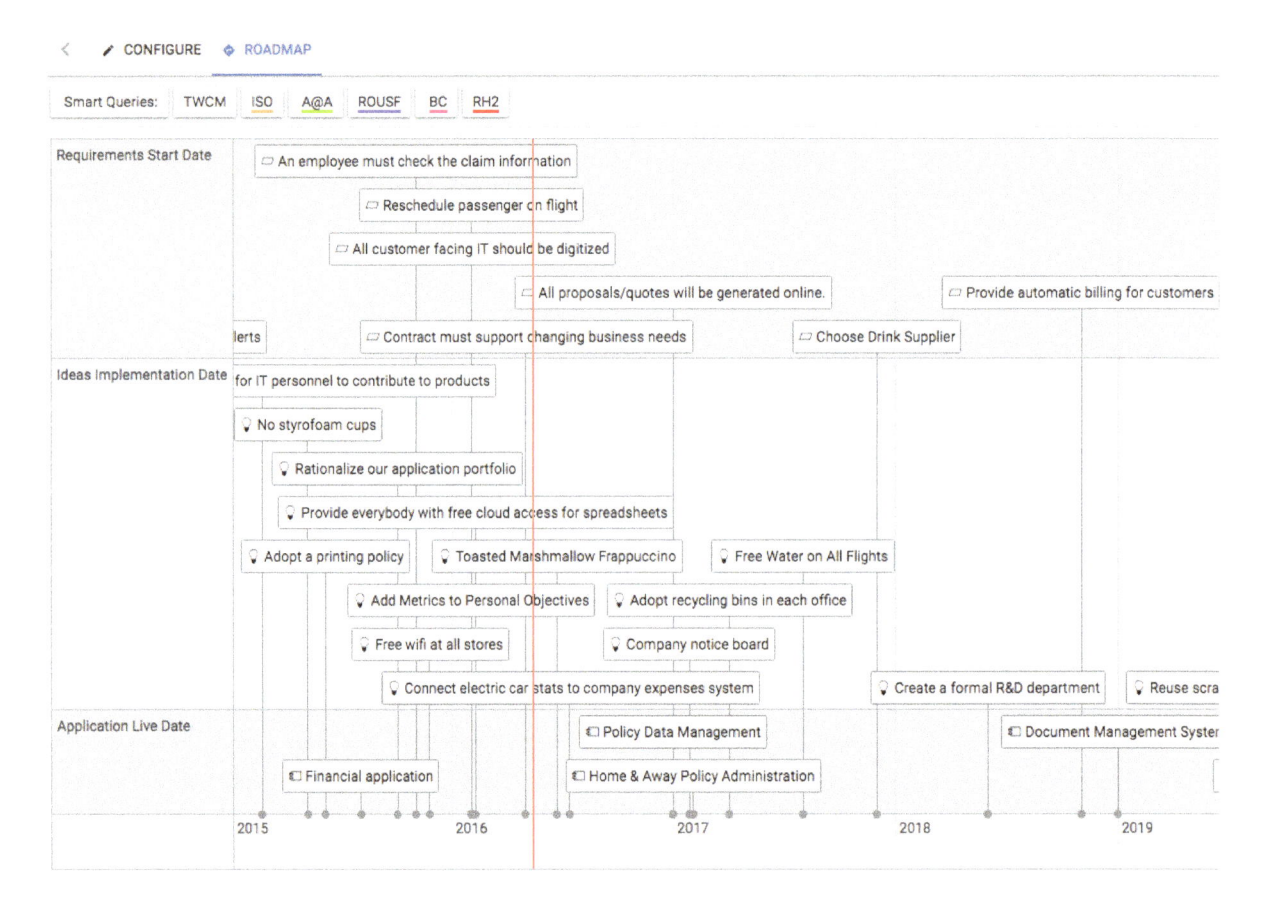

Figure 25: Roadmap with multiple meta-types

You can also add other types of concept into the lane. Notice in Figure 25, we have added requirements and their start dates and application components and the dates they are live. The different icons depict the different types.

The vertical red line is an indicator of todays date and is useful so that you can see where you are from a timing perspective in relation to today.

BASELINES

It is good practice to take snapshots of your roadmaps when decisions have been made.

Doing so, will allow you to compare the movement of the concepts on a roadmap over time, so you can see how your decision making has changed if you need to reflect back.

See the workspaces topic for more detail on baselines.

SUMMARY

Roadmaps provide a time-based view of a model. Whether you're using innovation management or enterprise architecture, a time based view of your concepts is essential for 'what if' analysis and planning future scenarios.

In different scenarios, the same set of concepts may have a different time visualization based on different time attributes.

Many organizations will have the concept of a lifecycle. It's important for companies to adopt a set of lifecycle states that have the same meaning across their stakeholders. For example, Sunset or End of Life but not both.

As roadmaps are always subject to change and are extremely volatile, then roadmap views should be generated automatically from the model. There should be little reason to create roadmaps without a model. They become extremely difficult to maintain and view in different ways later on.

CHAPTER 11

ANALYTICS AND DECISION MAKING

INTRODUCTION

This topic describes some of the tools and techniques that you will find useful in analyzing and making decisions about your architecture and innovation assets.

In this chapter, we're going to look at some ways to analyze and visualize your data in order to make decisions and demonstrate the economic benefits of innovation management and enterprise architecture.

OVERVIEW

Most organizations struggle to explain the value of their planning activities. Innovation management often stops at the prioritization of a good idea. Managers sometimes ask what Enterprise Architecture can do for them because it's not always obvious.

Making decisions by analyzing your architecture is important. This chapter does not intend to provide solutions for all of your analytics needs but to provide some examples and techniques that we've found useful.

The output of these techniques can be used as building blocks for any business case that is produced to justify a work package or initiative.

ANALYTICAL HIERARCHY PROCESS (PAIRWISE COMPARISON)

AHP OVERVIEW

The **analytic hierarchy process** (**AHP**) or **pairwise comparison** is a structured technique for organizing and analyzing complex decisions, based on mathematics and psychology.

It has particular application in group decision-making, and is used around the world in a wide variety of decision situations. In this book, we bring this technique into innovation management (IM) and enterprise architecture (EA) in order to allow communities to make decisions on complex concepts.

Instead of providing one unique decision, an AHP helps a group find a decision that maps to a particular goal or objective. The AHP is a framework for structuring a problem (based around decision making) and relating it to overall goals and providing solution alternatives.

This can apply to IM and EA in a number of ways:

- Comparing, ranking ideas against each other to work out the most suitable for a goal
- Ranking initiatives to see which has the most value
- Comparing workspaces or solution alternatives for the best option

In fact, any concept can be ranked and compared within the context of a suitable goal.

Users of the AHP first decompose their decision problem into hierarchy sub-criteria, each of which can be analyzed separately. The concepts within the hierarchy can relate to any aspect of the decision problem; tangible or intangible, carefully measured or roughly estimated, well or poorly understood—anything at all that applies to the decision at hand.

Once the AHP is built, the decision makers (users) systematically evaluate its various elements by comparing them to one another two at a time (Pairwise comparison), with respect to their impact on a concept (criteria) above them in the hierarchy. In making the comparisons, the decision typically use their judgments about the elements' relative meaning and importance. It is the fundamental foundation of the AHP technique that human decisions, and not just the underlying data, can be used in performing the evaluations.

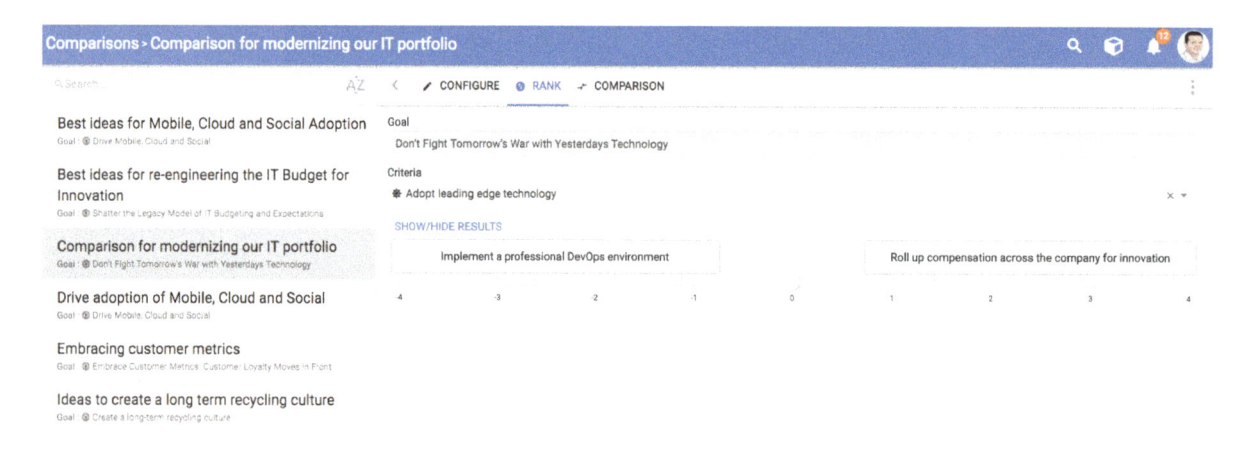

Figure 26: Pairwise comparison

It is typical that a question is defined at the criteria level of the hierarchy to guide the decision maker in making the qualitative assessment between the two concepts.

For example, "Which idea helps us get adoption for driving mobile, cloud and social in our company?"

The AHP framework provides a numerical value for each set of concepts that are part of a pairwise comparison. This technique allows diverse and often incommensurable elements to be compared to one another in a rational and consistent way. This capability distinguishes the AHP from other decision-making techniques.

Once all concepts have been compared, AHP provides an overall ranking for each concept with the context of the entire problem, for each of the decision alternatives. These numbers represent the alternatives' relative ability to achieve the goal, so they allow a straightforward consideration of the various courses of action.

Sum of Overall Priority	Criteria			
Alternatives	Close physical sales offices	Digitize account management	Provide customer self service	Grand Total
Build web portal	18.89	2.01	8.06	28.96
Digitize paper based accounts	13.42	2.81	6.52	22.75
Mobile platform for customer facing apps	3.38	0.34	0.85	4.57
New account application	36.97	1.84	4.91	43.72
Grand Total	72.66	7.00	20.34	100.00

USES AND APPLICATIONS

Although it has benefits for team decision-making, it can be used by individuals working on straightforward decisions. However, the Analytic Hierarchy Process (AHP) is definitely more beneficial where communities of people are working on complex problems.

It has unique advantages when important elements of the decision are difficult to quantify or compare, or where communication among team members is impeded by their different specializations, terminologies, or perspectives.

Decision situations to which the AHP can be applied include:

Choice – The selection of one alternative from a given set of alternatives, usually where there are multiple decision criteria involved.

Ranking – Putting a set of alternatives in order from most to least desirable

Prioritization – Determining the relative merit of members of a set of alternatives, as opposed to selecting a single one or merely ranking them

Resource allocation – Apportioning resources among a set of alternatives

Benchmarking – Comparing the processes in one's own organization with those of other best-of-breed organizations

Quality management – Dealing with the multidimensional aspects of quality and quality improvement

Conflict resolution – Settling disputes between parties with apparently incompatible goals or positions

The applications of AHP to complex decision situations have produced extensive results in problems involving planning, resource allocation, priority setting, and selection among alternatives.

For a detailed walkthrough of AHP, refer to the Appendix at the back of this book.

CHARTS AND INFOGRAPHICS

INTRODUCTION

Charts provide a graphical visualization of information. They are a useful communication mechanism for both technical and non-technical stakeholders.

OVERVIEW

Visualization of information in the correct format is critical to communicate with a broader audience.

As already covered, diagrams and models views are the key visualizations that enterprise architects expect to use. However, once model data is available, there are many different types of views that can be used.

Many people refer to charts and graphs as data visualization.

There are different types of graphical information. Quantitative and qualitative information.

We need both quantitative data and qualitative data in order to make decisions. Quantitative data is often the easiest to analyze and compute whilst qualitative data involves some human interpretation.

Quantitative information

Information that involves a measurement of any kind, typically taking a numerical form.

Examples are:

- Number of ideas generated for a campaign in Innovation Management
- Cost of application components over their lifetime in Enterprise Architecture
- Work package cost

Generally, it is fairly easy to compute this type of information. Numerical values lend themselves very well to traditional data visualizations.

Qualitative information

Anything non-numerical, this can involve both information and illustration.

Examples are:

- Business criticality: High, Medium or Low
- Business purpose
- Strategic objective

This type of information lends itself well to techniques such as infographics. Often, the information here is subjective and can be interpreted in different ways unless there is a strong commentary that belongs with it.

TRANSFORMING QUALITATIVE DATA INTO QUANTITATIVE DATA

To chart anything at all, we really need to provide a way for information to be transformed into computational values.

One approach, as In the AHP chapter, is to use techniques such as pairwise comparisons. These provide a mechanism for taking a qualitative assessment and producing a ranking, which is quantitative.

Arrays provide another manner in which to express qualitative data as a number.

We can use an array to express information with a corresponding numerical value. This value can then be used in charts and graphs to represent data.

Examples of arrays are:

- Requirement 'Business criticality': High: 100, Medium: 50, Low: 10
- Application 'Technical alignment': High: 100, Average: 60, Misaligned: 30, Not aligned: 1
- Idea 'Business benefit': Important': 100, Medium: 50, Negligible: 10

Each attribute has a list of pairs. Each pair consists of a textual name and a numerical value.

When an attribute has the value of the textual name, then its numerical value may be used to chart it in a graph.

It's very useful to always think about arrays from the outset of an innovation management and enterprise architecture initiative.

Even if you don't chart the attributes, you can always chart them later and may find arrays useful longer term.

A good tip is to ensure that you use a consistent scale across your model. In the examples above we used an upper limit of 100 and a lower limit of 1.
This ensures that your scales for charts are consistent across multiple attributes.

Scorecards provide a more advanced way of providing values and data that can be used in charts.

CHART TYPES

There are a number of chart types that you can use to visualize your data.

The different chart types will lend themselves well to different types of data depending on your communication needs.

In this section, we'll focus on three types; Bar charts, Scatter charts and Word clouds.

Bar chart

A **bar chart** or **bar graph** is a chart with rectangular bars with lengths proportional to the values that they represent. The bars can be plotted vertically or horizontally. A vertical bar chart is sometimes called a column bar chart.

A bar graph is a chart that uses either horizontal or vertical bars to show comparisons among categories. One axis of the chart shows the specific categories being compared, and the other axis represents a discrete value. Some bar graphs present bars divided into subparts to show cumulative effect (stacked bar graphs).

Values from concepts can represent either the whole stack or an element of the stack.

In Figure 27, the bar chart is stacked. The different colours of the stack represent different attribute values.

The range of concepts along the x-axis represents business processes. The y-axis represents the numerical value of each element in the stack. We can therefore see that the tallest concepts are those with the highest cumulative value.

For this example, its the action cost savings for applications that are associated with the business processes in our enterprise architecture.

Figure 28 uses the analytical hierarchy process (AHP) we defined earlier in the chapter to show the values of the priorities for each alternative and the criteria.

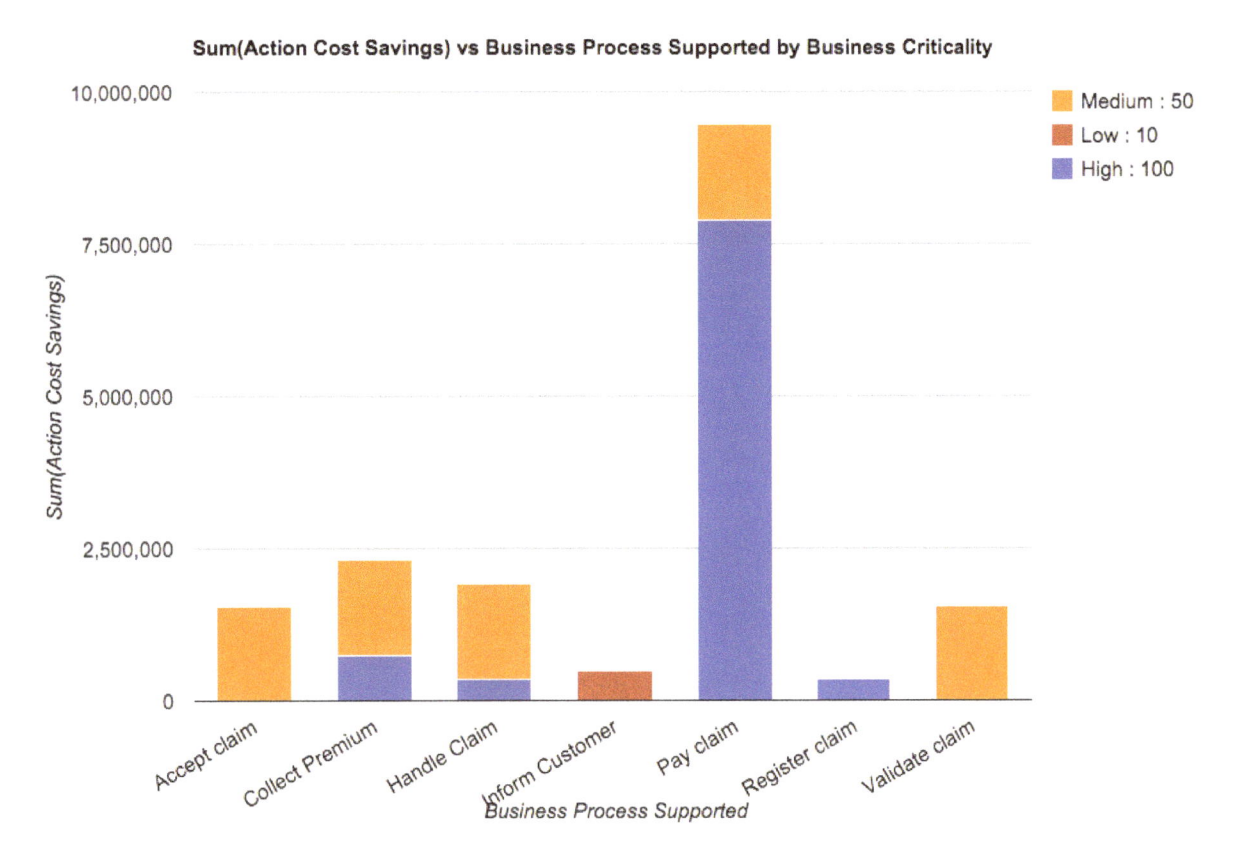

Figure 27: Stacked bar chart

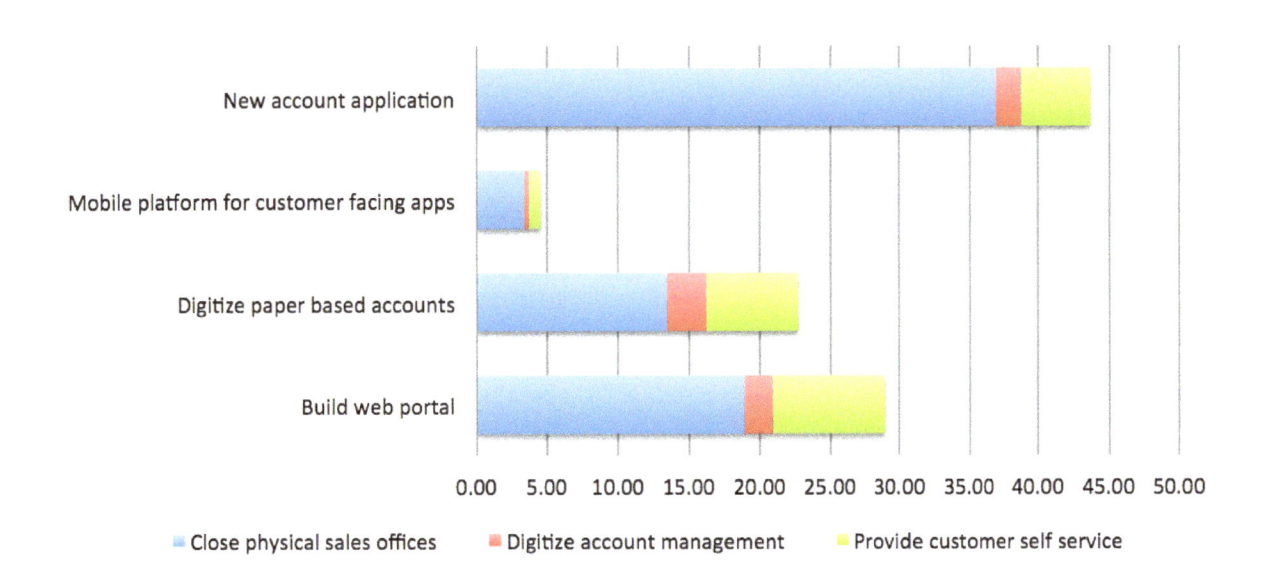

Figure 28: AHP results in stacked bar chart

Scatter chart

A **scatter chart** is a type of diagram using Cartesian coordinates to display values for two variables for a set of data.

The data is displayed as a collection of points, each having the value of one variable determining the position on the horizontal axis (x-axis) and the value of the other variable determining the position on the vertical axis (y-axis). This kind of plot is also called a *scatter plot*, *scatter gram*, *scatter diagram*, or *scatter graph*.

A scatter chart can also present z coordinates. At the intersection of the two points, further values can be displayed using shapes and colors.

A scatter chart is extremely useful for looking at correlations of data. For example, when looking for concepts with a high x and high y value, we can look in the top right hand corner of the chart to find them.

In Figure 29, we are showing applications and the attribute 'number of users' vs. the attribute 'active users', so we can see those applications that have more users than the number they are allocated. Each dot represents an application with those towards the upper left are those that we need to be aware of from an over usage perspective.

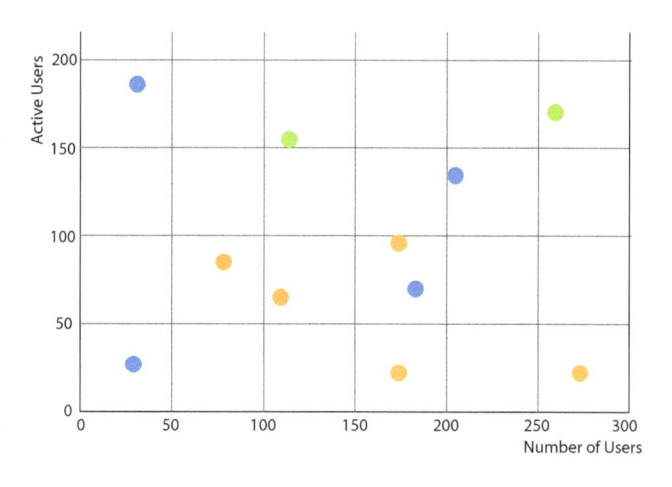

Figure 29: Scatter chart

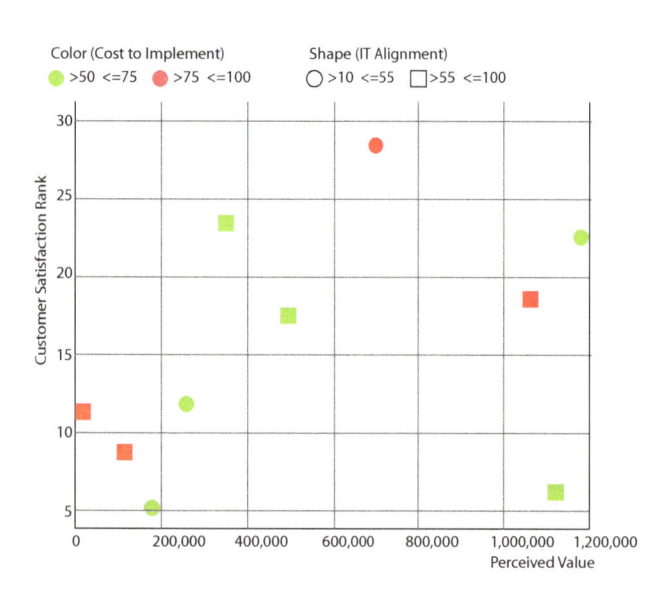

Figure 30: Ideas on a scatter chart

In Figure 30, a more complex example, we are showing ideas.

The y-axis is showing the customer satisfaction rank (from an AHP, as discussed previously) and the x-axis, the perceived value of the idea (as a currency value).

Thereby, we can see the ideas that are furthest to the top right have higher ranking and higher value and should be the ideas that we look to adopt.

Furthermore, this scatter chart has z attributes (as can be seen in the legend). The color of the concept is the cost to implement. Red being higher cost than green.

The shape of the concept represents the attribute of IT Alignment. A circle being low alignment and square high.

So, although it looks as though we should consider the idea on the far right upper quadrant of the chart, it actually has low IT alignment (circle) so may not align well with our IT strategy. Something we should examine.

As you can see, charts can really help with detailed analysis of our data. By representing data in different ways, we can start to look at different angles for decision-making.

Word clouds

A different type of chart is a word cloud. Word clouds can identify trends and patterns that would otherwise be unclear or difficult to see in a tabular format.

Frequently used keywords stand out better in a word cloud. Common words that might be overlooked in tabular form are highlighted in larger text making them pop out when displayed in a word cloud.

They can be an effective method for analysing text-data. The word cloud chart analyses the description contents of a meta-type and provides a summary of the keywords that are used.

Word clouds work well in ideation, when you want to explore campaigns and trending words and phrases within idea submissions. They provide insight into qualitative data.

Figure 31: Word cloud

Infographics

Although not the main topic of this chapter, we'll provide you with a brief overview of infographics here.

Infographic is an abbreviation of "Information Graphic". The term has gained popularity as marketing teams have increased their use of graphic to explain market messaging over the past few years.

Infographics are great for visual storytelling. They provide visual cues to communicate information. They are designed to be very light on data, don't need to be complex and don't need to be over analyzed.

Infographics are designed to leave viewers with a specific message to take away.

So why are infographics useful in innovation management and enterprise architecture?

So far, we've discussed quantitative data visualizations and how charts can visualize this information in an automated manner.

Infographics can be used to express both types of information.

You may use an Infographic to communicate the value of an ideation campaign and its results. Or you may decide to present enterprise architecture information through a narrative on an Infographic.

Other examples could be using an Infographic to communicate the value of your team or your project.

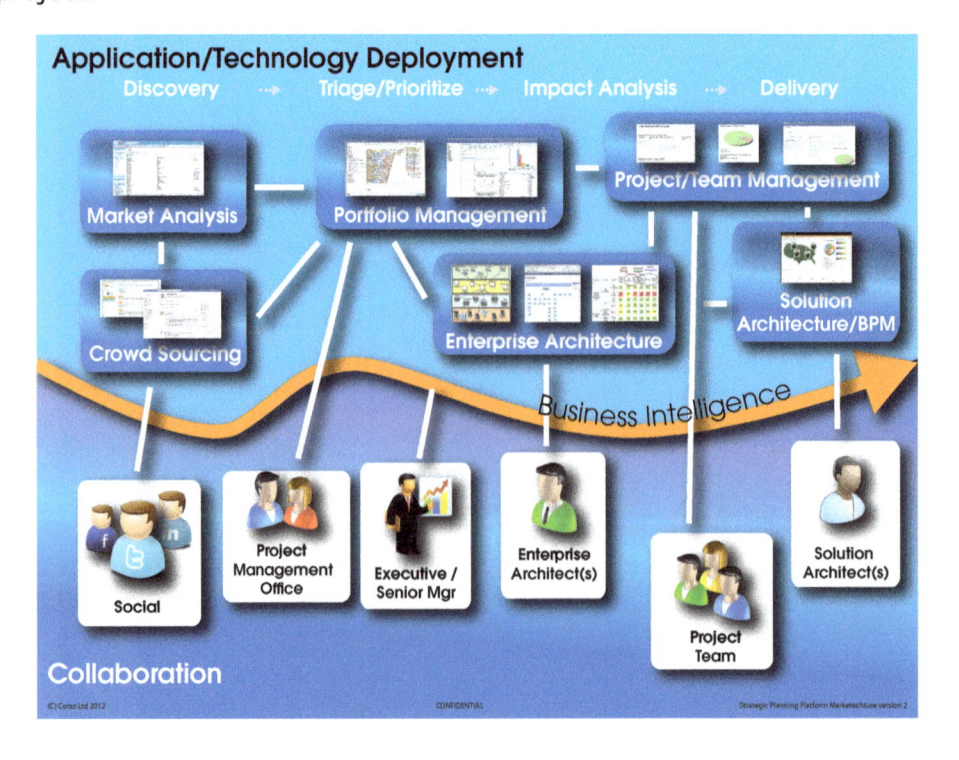

Figure 32: Example infographic

PIVOT TABLES

A pivot table is a data summarization tool. It is another form of data visualization.

Amongst its other functions, a pivot table can automatically filter, sort, group, count, average and perform other mathematical operations on data.

A major benefit of a pivot table is that is extremely quick and can be used to slice information through drag and drop.

Many of the attributes available to concepts lend themselves extremely well to data visualization and analysis of data. Each pivot table is for a given meta-type, e.g. Ideas or application components.

Pivot tables are an ideal tool to have in your kit bag for both innovation management and enterprise architecture.

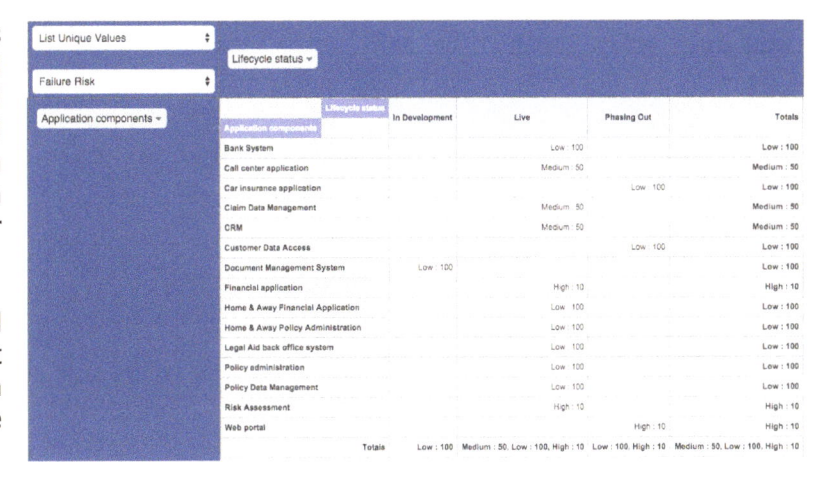

Figure 33: Pivot table

The table will help you identify and sort on patterns of information. For example, show me all of the applications, their lifecycles and place their 'failure risk' in the cells.

You can think of a pivot table as a visual and interactive report.

Most stakeholders can identify with pivot tables, as they will have seen them in spreadsheets in the past. Although readers of the pivot table may not be comfortable in creating them, they will certainly be adept at reading them.

A pivot table usually consists of row, column and data fields. You can interchange and swap column and row headers and group through drag and drop.

In Figure 34, we can see ideas, grouped by approval status in the rows and where the source has come from in the columns.

Data fields are where you can apply computational functions such as average, sum, total etc.

In this example we can see the perceived value of each idea and see the totals by source.

You will need to access a tool such as Corso's strategic planning platform to be able to automatically make use of model data in a pivot table.

HEATMAPS

A **heat map** is a graphical representation of data where the individual values are represented as colors. Heatmaps provide the ability to show any piece of the information with a color. The benefit being that we can immediately pick out the important data based on its color.

Figure 34: Ideas grouped by approval status

Heatmaps don't require the use of colors and rely on the changing of fonts, shapes and visual structure to represent data. But when used they often use this universal scheme.

Heatmaps are excellent communication aids to allow other stakeholders to see the important data. Heatmaps are usually used with views.

Charts and graphs are one type of analytic that may use colors and shapes to define Heatmaps. Diagrams may have their shapes colored to reflect data values and of course we saw in figvre 34, a Pivot Table with a heat map.

More complex Heatmaps involve the roll-up of data so we can see the impact of values against other parts of architecture or innovation. For example, we could show the business capabilities with the most ideas generated for them. The business capability map would show the capabilities with the most ideas in green scaling to red for the least.

SCORECARDS

In a similar manner in which a spreadsheet allows a user to define calculations on cells, scorecards provide a similar capability. Scorecards help you manage and evaluate metrics that can be applied to concepts. With many concepts, creating an automated score is the best way to calculate value.

Scorecards (sometimes called custom attributes) should appear as attributes within a concept. Scorecards may be assigned to different Meta-types.

For example, a scorecard might use a person's age, credit rating and employment status to calculate the person's final score. Figure 35, shows how this scorecard is calculated from the four attributes (metrics) represented as slider bars using the formula (attribute 1 + attribute 2 + attribute 3 + attribute 4)/4.

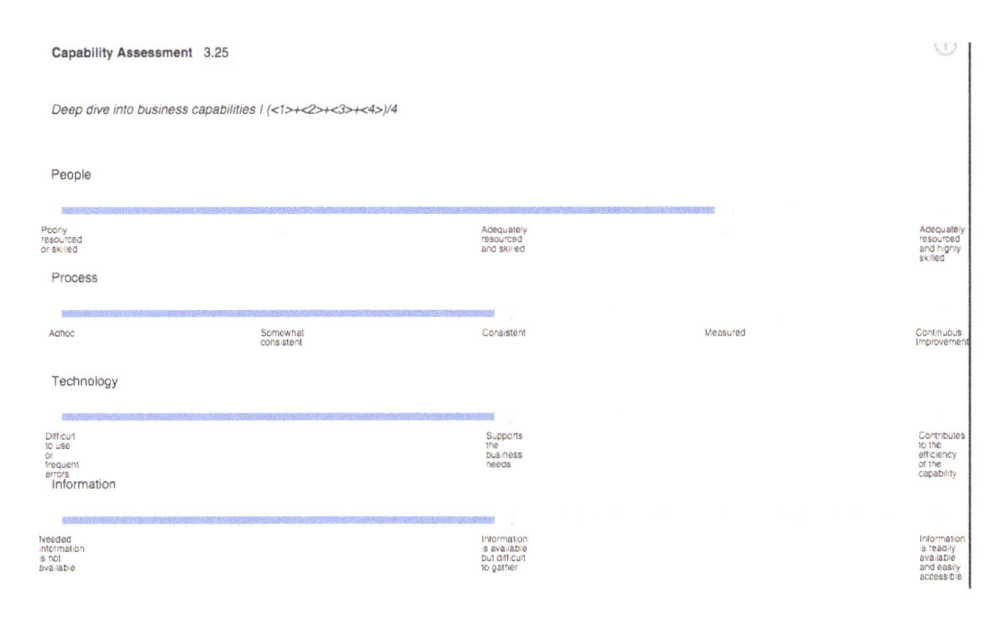

Figure 35: Example scorecard for business capability

Scorecards are extremely powerful for analyzing existing attributes and providing a score.

We could provide a capability assessment in the organization and rate the people, processes, technology and information characteristics.

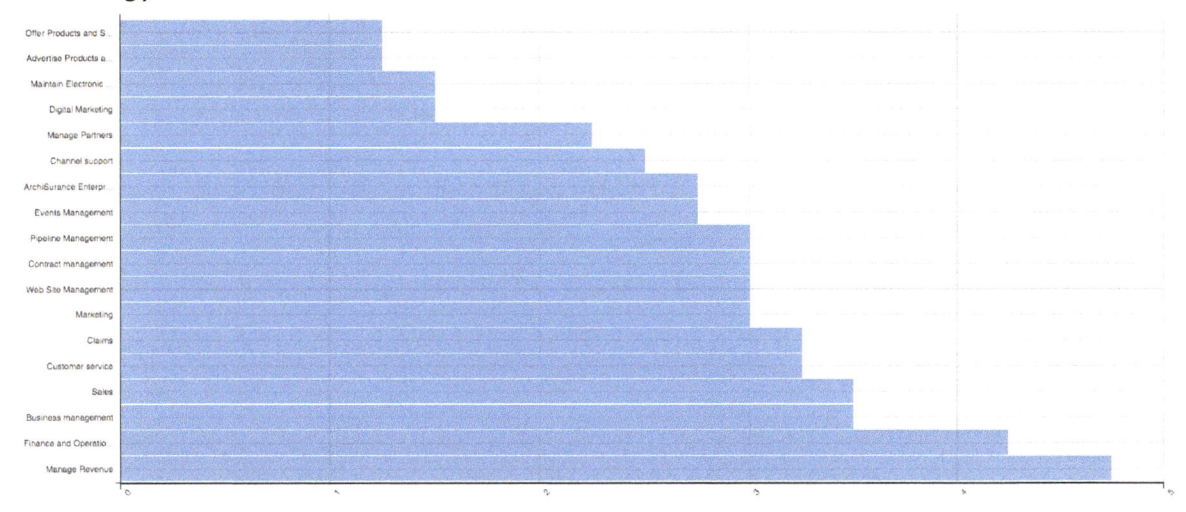

Figure 36: Chart showing values of business capability assessment

All four of these values provide a Capability Assessment Value. In the example in figure 35 it is 3.25.

You can then use standard views such as Pivot Tables and Charts to analyze the output.

SCORECARD ATTRIBUTES

Metrics can be made up of other attributes. It may be useful to tie the value of an existing attribute in a meta-type to a metric value.

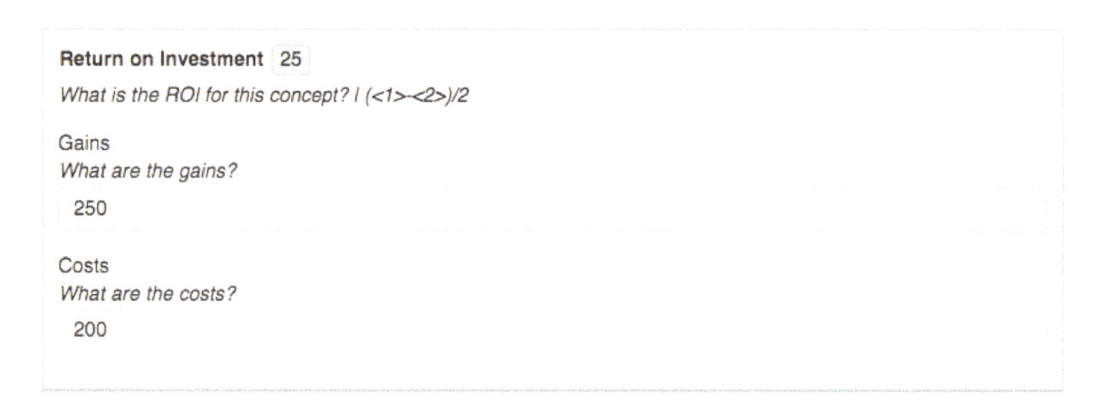

Figure 37: Example scorecard for return on investment (ROI)

In Figure 37, we can see that the Expected Cost is 200. The gains are 250, therefore the Return on Investment (ROI) value (250-200)/2 for a total of 0.25 or 25%.

EXAMPLES OF SCORECARDS

Scorecards for Innovation Management

Scorecard – Innovation Score

Attractiveness – High = 10, Medium = 5, Low = 1
Time to Market – 1 Month = 10, 2-6 Months = 8, 6-12 Months = 6, 1-2 Years = 4, 2-3 Years = 2, 3 Years+ = 1
Anticipated Risk – High = -5, Medium = -3 Low = -1

Development Effort – High = -10, Medium = -5, Low = -1
Increase in Brand Value

Innovation Score = 1 x Attractiveness x 1 x Time to Market x 1 x Anticipated Risk x 1 x Development Effort x 1 x Increase in Brand Value

Scorecard – Requirements Score

Resources Required - High = 10, Medium = 5, Low = 1
Resource Experience rating

Business Alignment - High = 10, Medium = 5, Low = 1

IT Alignment - High = 10, Medium = 5, Low = 1
Project costs – High = -10, Medium = -5, Low = -1

Requirements Score = 1 x (Resources Required / Resource Experience Rating) x 1 x Business Alignment x IT Alignment x Project Costs

Scorecard - Marketing Score

Brand Impact
Word of Mouth Potential
Fits customer demographic
Case studiable (weighting x 2)

Marketing Score = 1 x Brand Impact x 1 x Word of Mouth Potential x 1 x Fits customer demographic x (2 x Case studiable)

Examples of scorecards are also available in the Portfolio Management section of this book.

SUMMARY

Analytic tools are necessary to drive out decision making from your concepts.

We've covered different types of analytics tools in this chapter ranging from pairwise decision making to visualizing data with charts and Heatmaps.

We've also covered different types of data such as quantitative and qualitative data and different ways to view this information and make use of it.

In general, you will use a combination of these types of tools and data to analyze your architecture at its current state.

You can also use these techniques as part of driving out the business benefit of your architecture for further investment by the business or to compare two workspaces.

CHAPTER 12

WORK PACKAGES AND PROJECTS

INTRODUCTION

This topic discusses the concept of work packages. Work packages are extremely important as they detail the work to be done in order to deliver something. Whether working in innovation management and/or enterprise architecture, work packages provide the context for getting things done.

OVERVIEW

In general project management terms, a work package is often viewed as a subset of a project.

In ArchiMate®, a central concept is a work package. It is part of the implementation and migration extension. In this book, we refer to a work package in the ArchiMate® sense. It has a clearly defined start and end date, and has a set of well defined goals and deliverables.

The work package can represent any of the following types of work (and others):

- Epic - a large body of work that can be broken down into a number of smaller stories
- Initiative - work that is substantial in scope as to warrant up-front (ROI) analysis
- Portfolio - the collection of all work initiatives including roles and resources
- Program - a package of work that is beyond the remit of one project and one team
- Project - a planned set of interrelated activities to be executed over a fixed period and within certain cost and other limitations usually with a deliverable/outcome
- Spike - a task aimed at answering a question rather than producing a product
- Sprint - an uninterrupted period of time during which a team performs work and produces a deliverable
- Story - describes a desired capability/requirement from a users point of view
- Work package - a set of activities that realize requirement(s) and produces deliverables

From the work package categories, we can have hierarchical work packages. For example a program of work can decompose into a project and a project into a series of sprints.

A work package is a series of tasks that are designed to achieve a goal within a set period of time.

Work packages produce deliverables that should be of some business benefit.

Work packages also include budgets, resource and costs allocated to them.

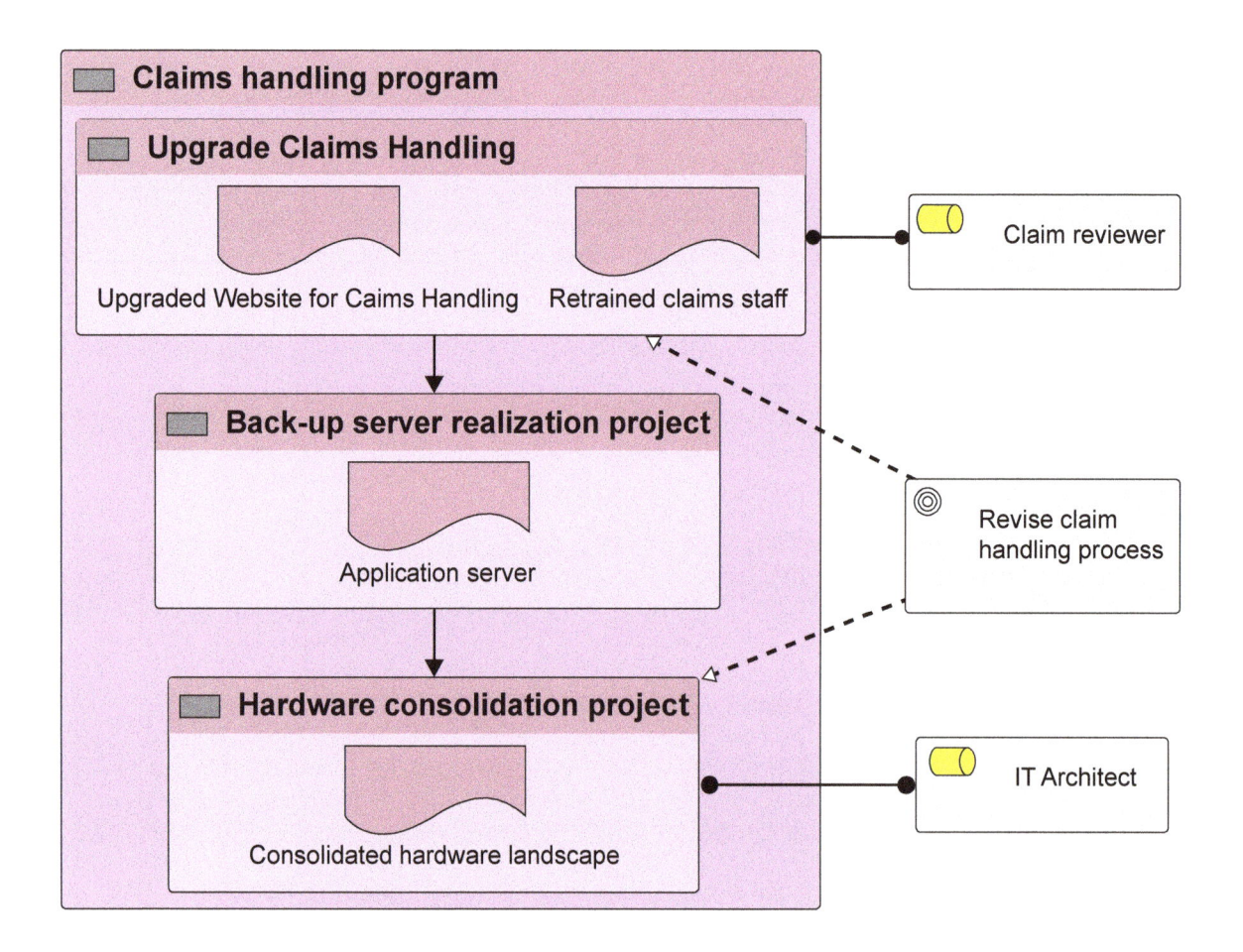

Figure 38: ArchiMate project view

Consider the ArchiMate® Project View in Figure 38. It shows a Claims handling program, which consists of three projects: Upgrade Claims Handling, Back-up server realization project and Hardware consolidation project. You can see the order of the projects and the goals they achieve.

For each project, you can see the set of expected deliverables.

Where roles are assigned to projects, you can see these.

DETAIL AND TECHNIQUES

There are various approaches to managing work packages including Agile, Lean and Prince2.

Agile management is an iterative and incremental method of managing work packages. It is based around creating small increments of deliverables and includes other stakeholders such as customers and users.

Lean management is the method used to plan and implement a lean project. Sometimes users of lean practices follow the 6-sigma DMAIC method or use the Deming cycle.

PRINCE2 (an acronym for PRojects IN Controlled Environments) is a de facto process-based method for effective project management. Used extensively by the UK Government, PRINCE2 is also widely recognized and used in the private sector, both in the UK and internationally.

Most techniques use the concept of a work package (project) within the context of their own framework. All of these techniques have participants and roles.

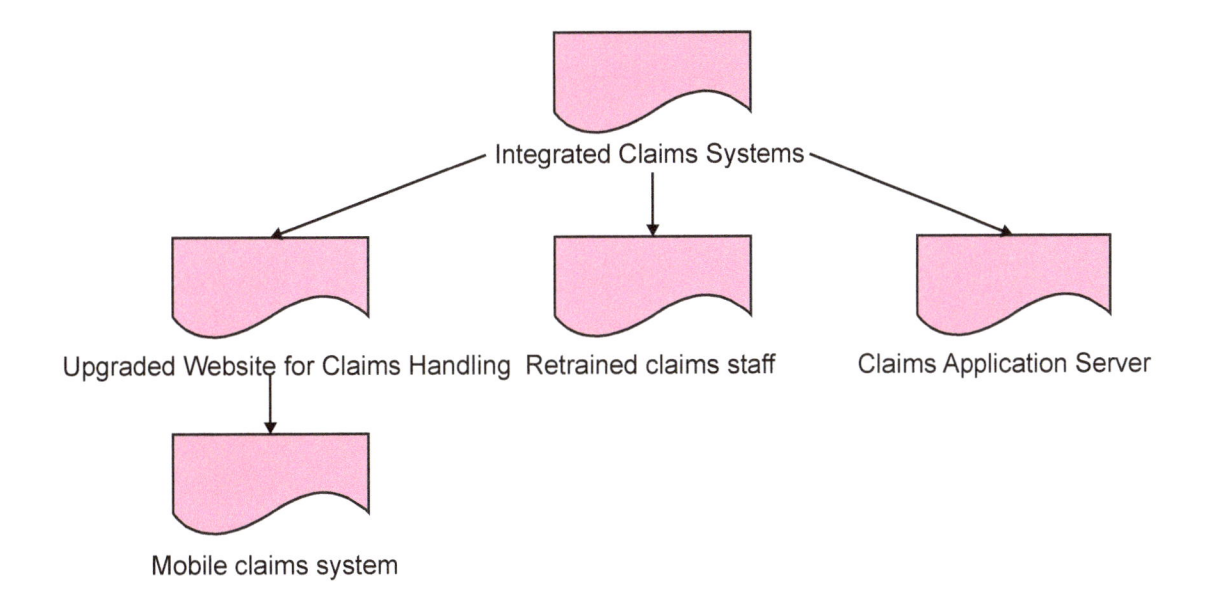

Figure 39: Work product breakdown structure

In PRINCE2, the overall result of a project is described in a 'project product description'; the hierarchical decomposition of this product into sub-products is shown in a product breakdown structure. Product breakdown structures are represented in ArchiMate® as deliverables with composition or aggregation associations. Projects produce deliverables.

ROLES AND STAKEHOLDERS

There are typical work package roles that exist for projects. These include:

- **Project Manager** – is usually a professional in the field of project management. Project managers can have the responsibility of the planning, execution, and closing of any project, whether based around innovation management, enterprise architecture or portfolio management

- **Project Stakeholders** – are those people within an enterprise that sponsor a project or, have an interest or a gain upon a successful completion of the goals of a project.

- **Project Team** – is the management team leading the project, and provide services to the project.

- **Project Management Office** – The PMO in an enterprise is the group that defines and maintains the standards of process, generally related to project management, within the organization. The PMO strives to standardize and manage the commercials of the execution of projects. The PMO is the source of documentation, guidance and metrics on the practice of project management and execution.

Stakeholders and roles can be modelled with ArchiMate.

When defining Kanban boards, it's useful to assign the roles of users to the stages of the Kanban, so that they become part of the workflow.

RISK REGISTER

A risk register is a risk management tool commonly used in risk management and compliance. It acts as a central repository for all risks identified by the organization and, for each risk, includes information such as source, nature, treatment option, existing counter-measures, recommended counter-measures and so on. It can sometimes be referred to as a risk log (for example in PRINCE2).

Risk registers are normally associated with a work package or project. They help catalogue and quantify any risks for the project. They are reviewed at project meetings and stand ups.

INNOVATION MANAGEMENT AND WORK PACKAGES

Work packages can be created to manage work for moving ideas through the innovation funnel. A campaign is the place-holder for concepts related to an innovation challenge. It is natural to have work packages created to handle the decision-making and justification of high value ideas.

Ideas and requirements stemming from ideation can also be assigned to work packages. A work package may span the entire ideas to delivery framework and involve many stakeholders.

In Figure 40, Upgrade Claims Handling is associated with the *Automatically pay claims <$1000* idea and *All claims shall be submitted online* requirement.

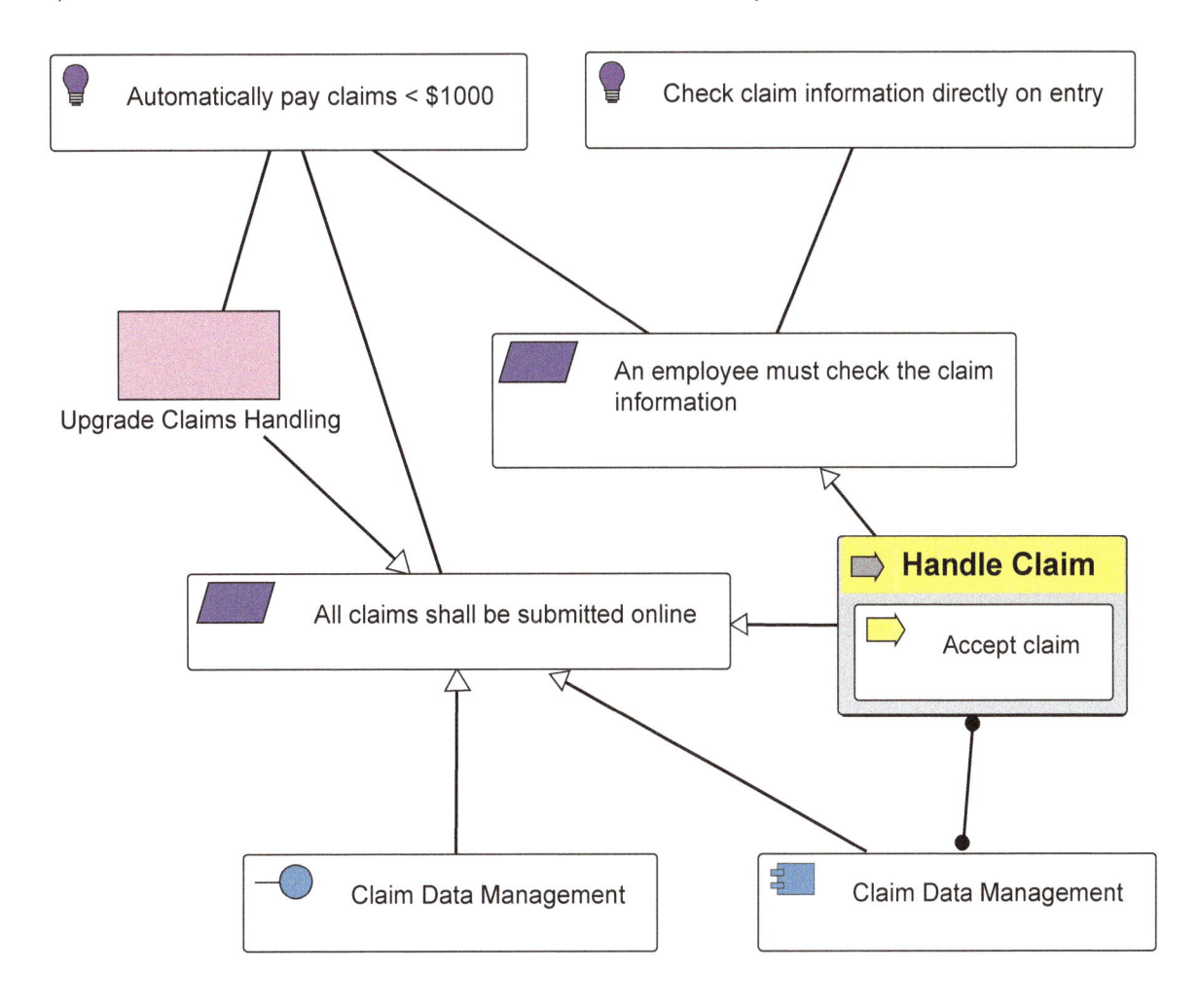

Figure 40: Idea to delivery viewpoint

ENTERPRISE ARCHITECTURE AND WORK PACKAGES

A work package consists of a set of related tasks, aimed at producing a well-defined result.

Architecture change requires work packages to drive it. Work packages representing programs and projects can be associated with the parts of the architecture that they implement. The work package allows an architect to scope the programs, projects and project activities that are realized by workspaces (plateaus) or the individual architecture concepts that are affected.

Work packages provide the bridge between Enterprise Architecture and Portfolio Management.

Using enterprise architecture, it is possible to analyze potential overlap between work package activities or to analyze the consistency between project dependencies and dependencies among workspaces (plateaus) or architecture elements.

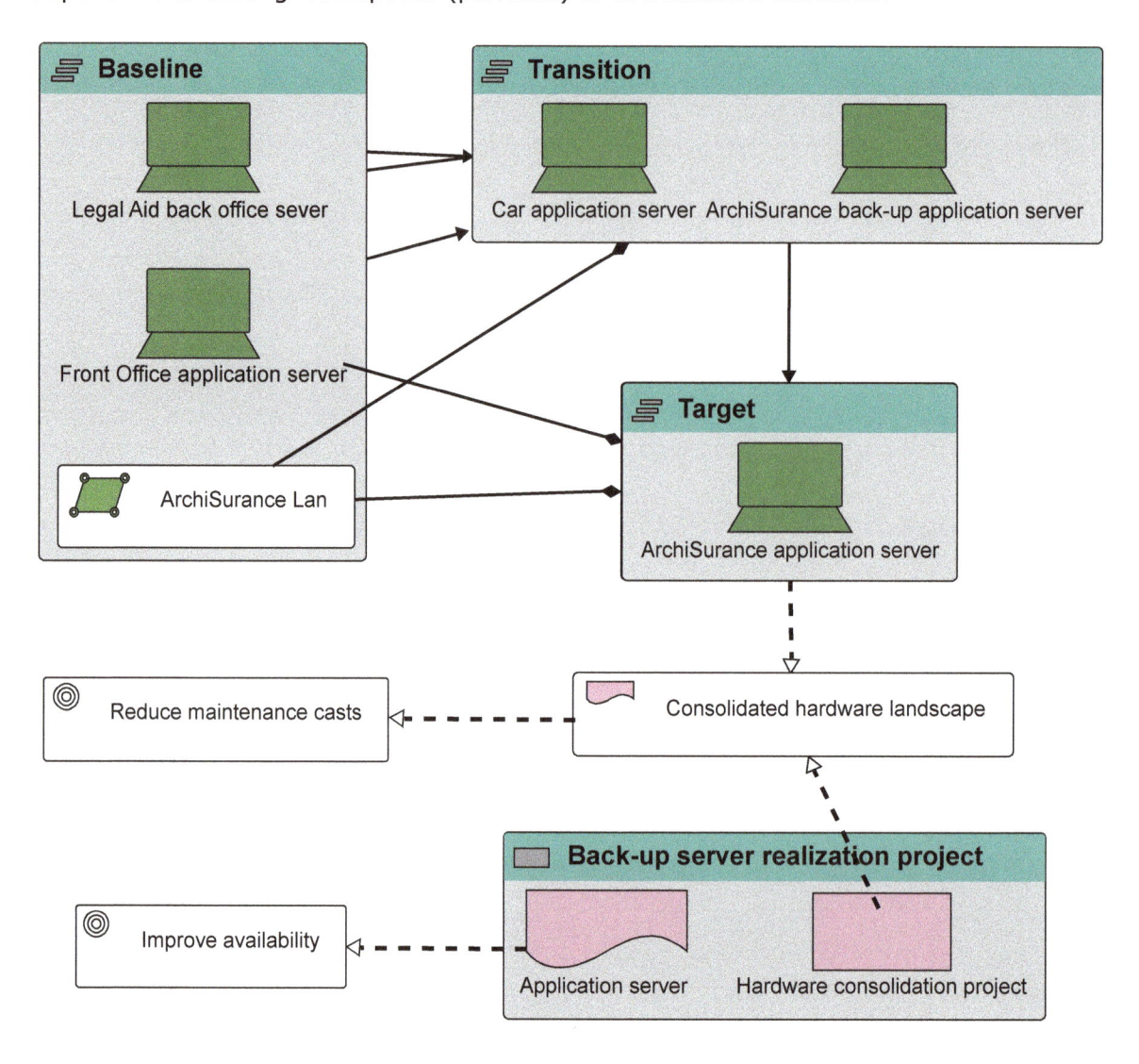

Figure 41: Implementation and migration viewpoint

The ArchiMate® implementation and migration viewpoints provide diagrammatic representation of work packages and associated meta-types.

SUMMARY

A work package is an endeavour undertaken to create a result that provides benefit. The temporary nature of work packages dictates that a work package has a definite beginning and end. The end is reached when the project's objectives have been achieved or when the project is terminated because its objectives will not or cannot be met, or when the need for the project no longer exists.

Project management is the application of knowledge, skills, tools, and techniques to project activities to meet the work package requirements. Project management is accomplished through the appropriate application and integration of the following project management process groups:

- Initiating
- Planning
- Executing
- Monitoring and Controlling
- Closing

Managing a work package typically includes, but is not limited to:

Identifying needs and requirements;

Addressing the various needs, concerns, and expectations of the stakeholders in planning and executing the work package;

Setting up, maintaining, and carrying out collaboration among stakeholders

Guiding stakeholders towards meeting work package requirements and creating work package deliverables;

Balancing the competing work package constraints, which include, but are not limited to:

- Scope
- Quality
- Schedule
- Budget
- Resources
- Risks

The specific work package characteristics and circumstances can influence the constraints on which the project management team needs to focus.

The ArchiMate® motivation extension provides a meta-model and meta-types that support the motivational elements of work packages.

CHAPTER 13

WORKSPACES AND VERSIONING

This topic addresses the capabilities and requirements for workspaces & versioning, which are important when understanding and mapping out the near and long term strategy for any initiative.

OVERVIEW

When envisioning and planning out any initiative, especially and architectural driven one, its important to keep an overall enterprise blueprint (model) up to date and maintained. Various initiatives and plans may impact upon the blueprint over its lifetime.

As a business evolves, then so does its architecture. A strategy for maintaining the architecture over its lifetime (the baseline) is important to allow change to be driven in the context of everything else.

DETAIL AND TECHNIQUES

There are a number of techniques that are necessary to manage architecture over time. These include:

Understanding the enterprise baseline, workspaces, baselines, merge and extract, workspace compare, concept versioning, concept compare and communities.

The following sections detail each of these topics and why they are important and how they work together.

DEALING WITH CHANGE

When we look at change within the context of innovation management and/or enterprise architecture, we can see that change is continuous, slower (than change in software development) and often has a medium-high approval cycle (governance).

There is also a need to manage access to information through community groups so that some aspects of the detail cannot be changed or viewed without permission.

Proposals for change can take the form of multiple plans, options and programs that are proposed.

One of the main deliverables for an architecture blueprint is a set of recommendations and constraints and some idea of how to transition and decide between blueprints and different alternatives.

The outputs of these alternatives maybe Time lines/Roadmaps, costs and resource.

An organization may move through different lifecycles at different phases of their enterprise architecture practice.

For example, within the TOGAF ADM, different iterations and approval lifecycles may be carried out.

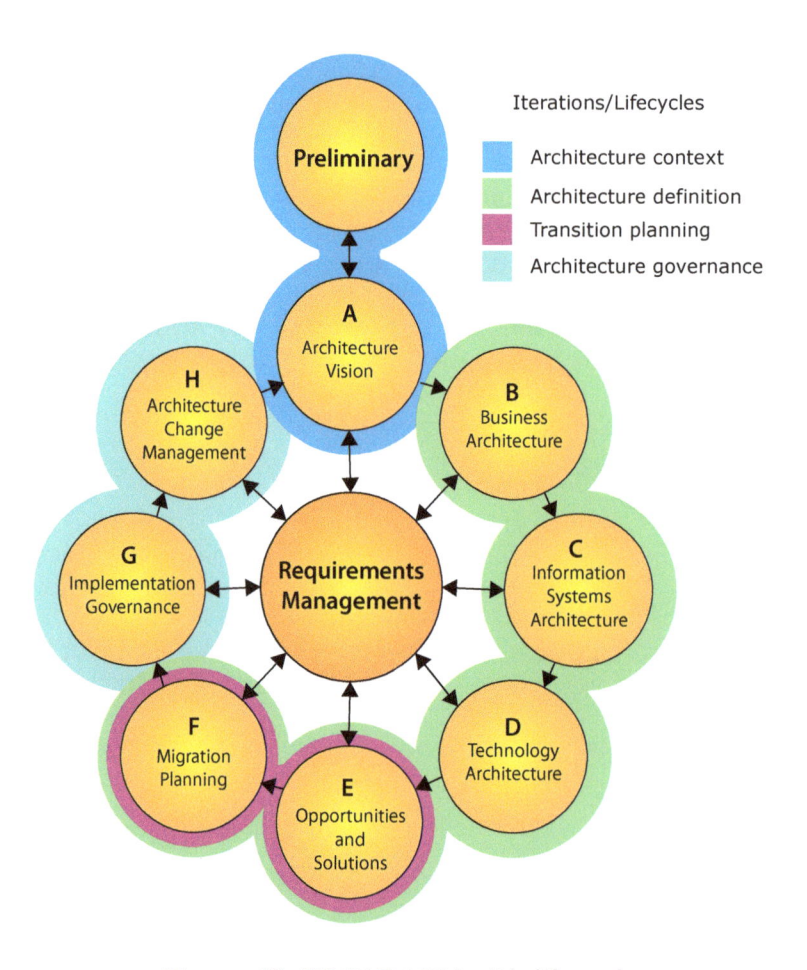

Figure 42: TOGAF ADM with lifecycles

Architecture context is setting the context of the architecture initiative. Architecture definition is about defining and iterating through the domains of architecture. Transition planning is focusing on moving from one state of the architecture to another. And, Architecture governance is about applying management and sign-off activities to architecture initiatives.

ENTERPRISE BASELINE

As an organization matures its architecture over time, a published version of the architecture should be made available. This will normally be done as a major release.

An enterprise baseline is a continuous moving target, in TOGAF term the continuum. That is, we would never roll back to a baseline without losing all of the descendants of the baseline. It is best practice to create a copy of a workspace of the baseline and increment that with a major version number.

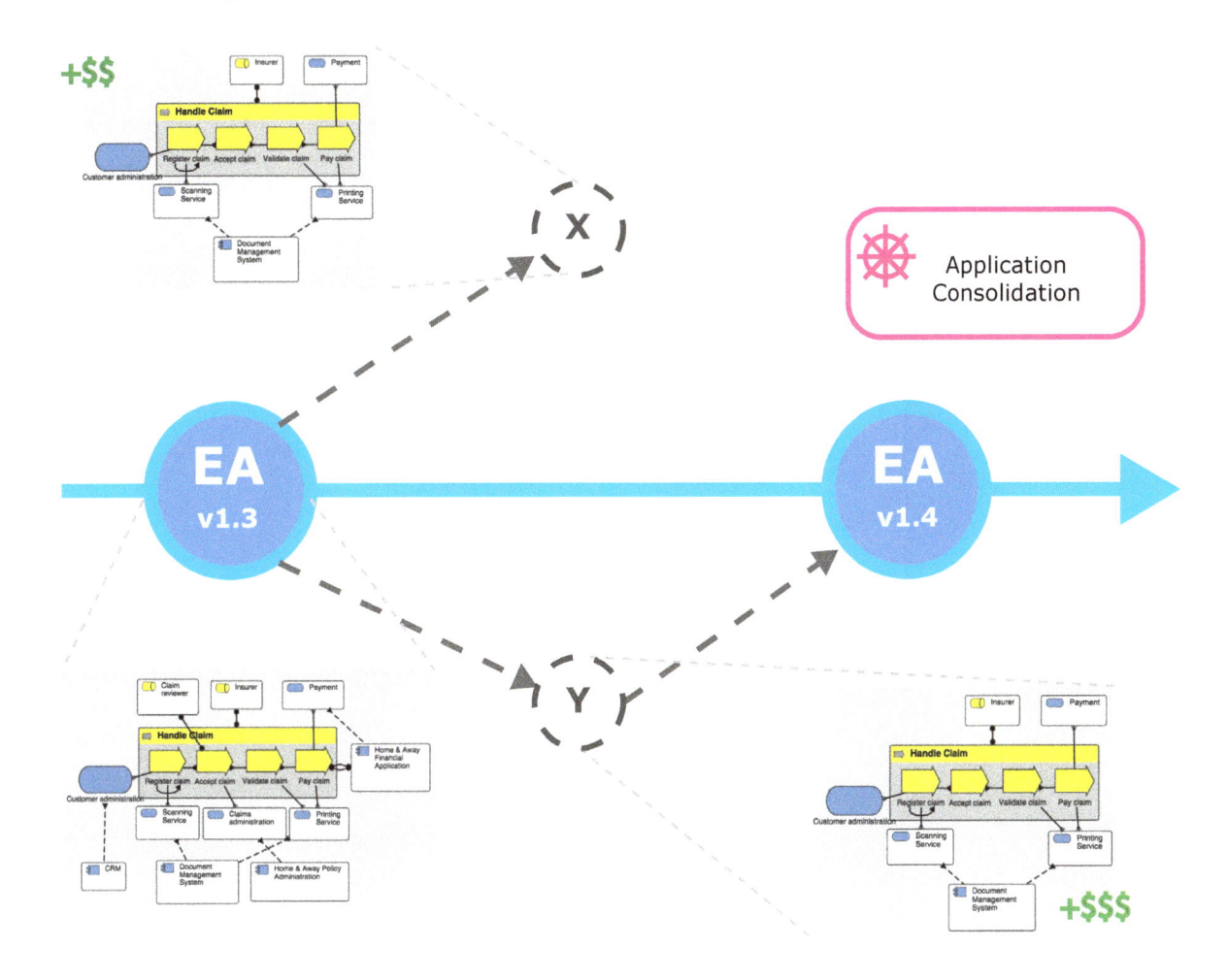

Figure 43: "as is" and "to be" workspaces

In a simple 'as is' and 'to be' scenario (Figure 43), we may decide to outsource some of our data and systems management. Two alternative architectures may be examined and one chosen as the outcome.

Whilst alternative X and Y may be compared for value, the current architecture is baselined.

When Y is chosen, it becomes the new baseline. This is an extremely simple way of managing architecture.

At this point, we can publish the new baseline to the organization.

However, in most instances, management of the baseline and alternatives are far more complex.

Figure 44 shows some example implementation and migration patterns for innovation management and enterprise architecture.

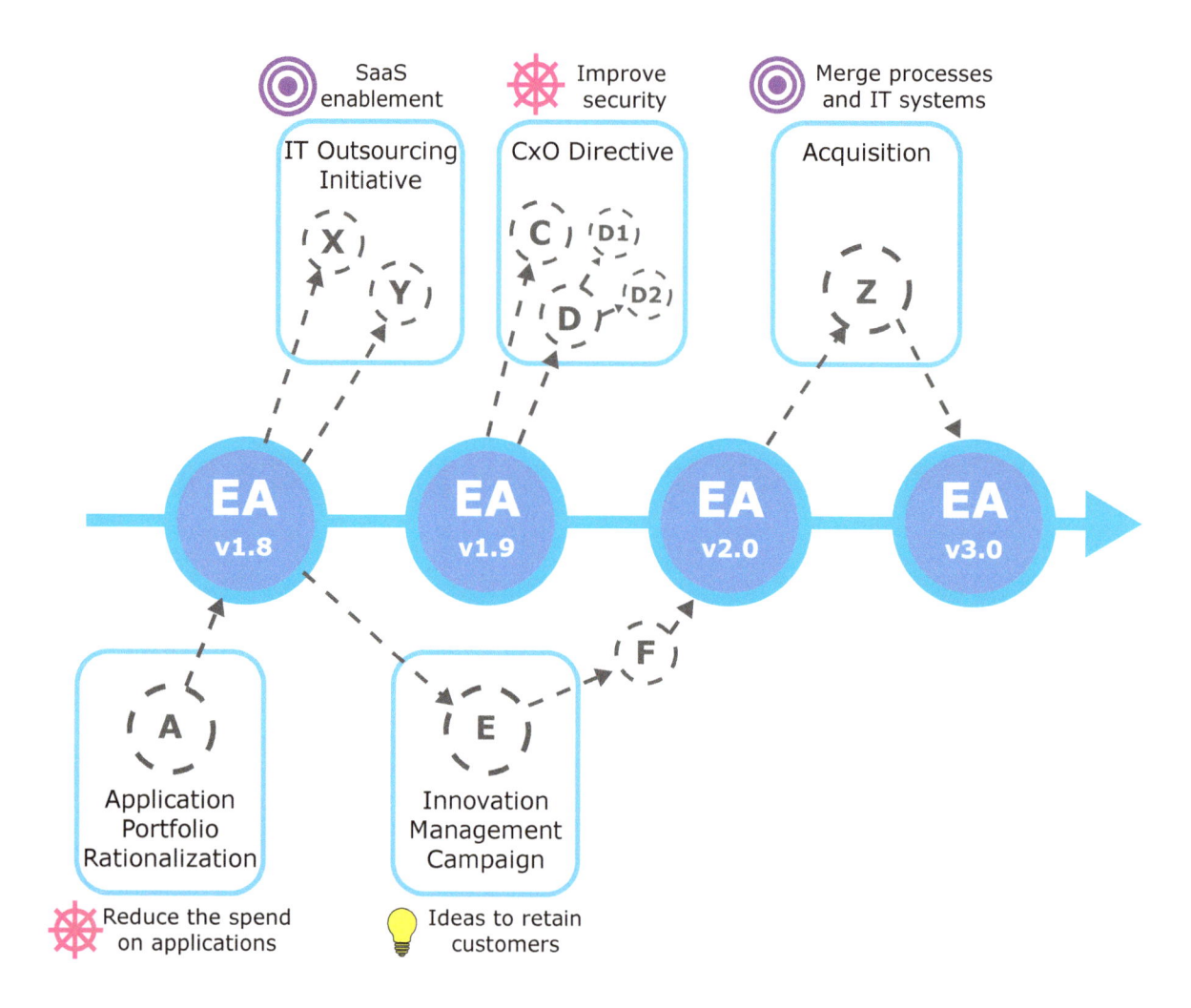

Figure 44: Implementation and migration patterns

WORKSPACES

Workspaces can equate to the Plateau concept in ArchiMate. However, we've used the term workspace as it has a wider meaning.

A workspace is defined as a relatively stable state of the architecture that exists at a moment in time.

A workspace can represent either current, future or transition architecture. By nature, workspaces are hierarchical.

Transition workspaces represent the enterprise at incremental states reflecting the periods of transition between a current and future architecture (sometimes called baseline and target architecture). A current and future architecture may have many transition workspaces between them showing alternative ways that a future architecture may be achieved.

Transition workspaces are used to allow for work packages and projects to be grouped into managed portfolios and programs, demonstrating the business value of each transition.

Workspaces should be created from other workspaces to create hierarchies and lineage.

In this manner, workspaces can be used for decision making about alternatives.

BASELINES

When a workspace exists for a limited time and is unlikely to be changed, we can baseline the architecture. Once architecture has been baselined, it should not be modified again, instead, it should flow to new target architecture. All changes should be made in the target architecture.

You should be able to view any baseline for historical purposes and to compare to the any other workspace.

MERGE AND EXTRACT

In order to copy concepts between workspaces, its important to be able to merge into your current workspace or to extract out of your current workspace.

Each concept you define should have a unique identifier. The identifier shouldn't be the name.

When a concept is copied to another workspace (or made available to a workspace), it should retain its lineage.

Workspaces that are baselined cannot have concepts copied into them.

LINEAGE, WORKSPACE COMPARE AND GAPS

When a concept exists within multiple workspaces, and the lineage has been created from workspace to workspace, then a compare can take place between two or more workspaces.

Lineage is an extremely important concept. Much like human ancestors have lineage (grand parents, children, siblings etc.), concepts can have lineage.

The lineage is maintained through a concepts identifier. This means that even if a concept changes name between workspaces, we can still compare the concept by tracing its lineage up and down the workspace hierarchy.

A gap is the difference between two workspaces or plateaus. A gap usually shows what was created, updated or deleted between two workspaces. A gap is closely tied to a work package as it may instantiate a set of work to be done.

A comparison between two workspaces can automatically produce the contents of the gap and the created, updated or deleted status of the gap. Again this helps with project and portfolio management when assessing initiatives and work.

CONCEPT VERSIONING

Concepts within their own right may be versioned. When a new version of a concept is produced, the current version of the concept is baselined. The concept baseline stores all of the associations that the concept currently has in that version, including the destination concepts at the end of an association.

Version numbers are incremental and usually system generated.

A user may work on the current version and can see the previous versions for reference purposes.

A model is a network of concepts and other concepts will have their own associations. The current version of a concept only includes its immediate relatives. This is very similar to a configuration set in version control systems.

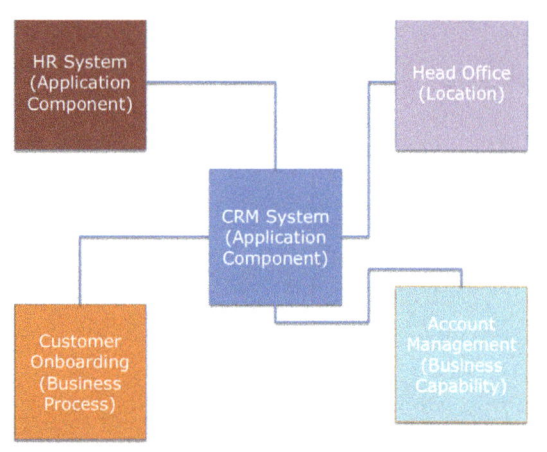

Figure 45: Version 1 of CRM system and its associations

In a team environment, concepts that are related via other concepts may well have been changed at a different time, in a different workspace or completely removed.

In Figure 46, we can see that the account management business capability has its own set of associations but these are not part of the CRM System version.

If a concept version is rolled back to a previous version then all of its immediate relatives are rolled back to but not their associations.

If a concept has been removed, it is put back in place. If an association was removed it is added back.

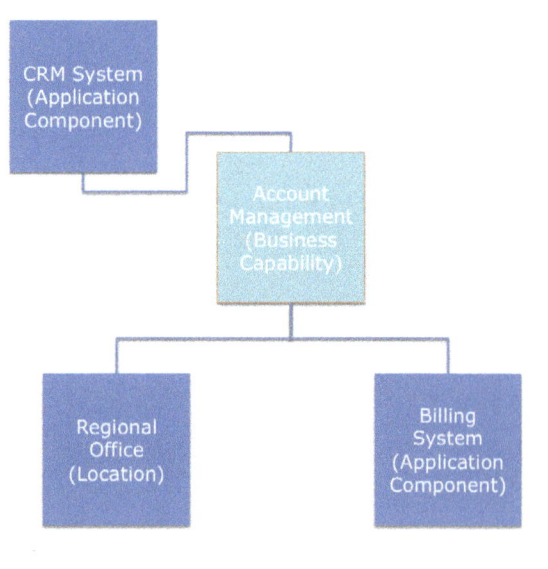

Figure 46: Business capability and its associations

The implication of this is that rolling back a version of a concept may change the semantic meaning of the overall model as in Figure 47.

In Figure 48, Account Management had Account Manager associated with it.

If CRM System is rolled back to version 1 from version 2, then the new model looks like this example.

There is a balance between base lining workspaces (entire configuration sets) and individual concepts.

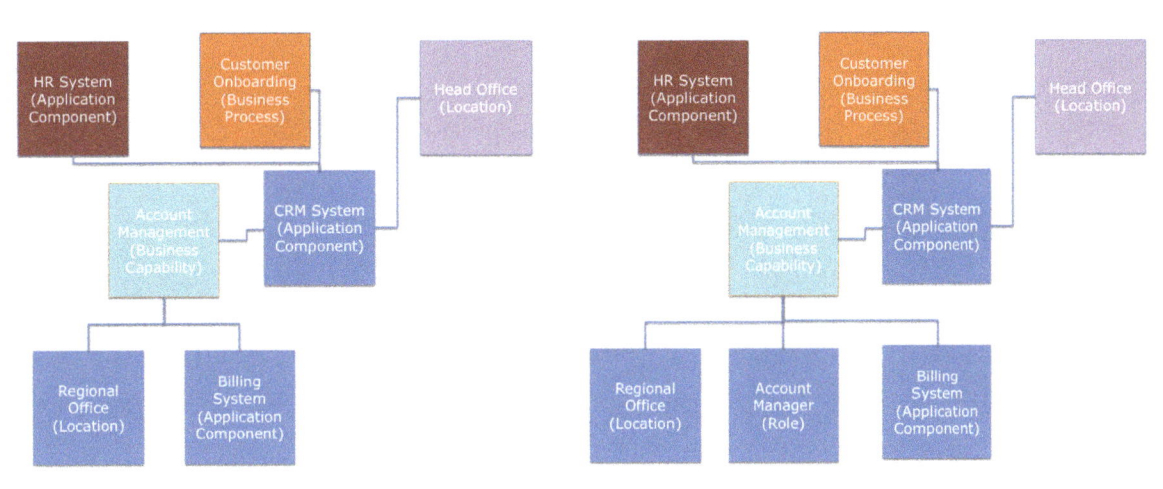

Figure 47: Rolled back CRM system

Figure 48: Rolled back CRM system with modified siblings

CONCEPT COMPARE

It is useful just to compare the lineage of a single concept anywhere.

Where used

In its simplest form, a 'where used' report is useful to show which concepts are in which workspaces and what their version numbers are. This report also makes use of lineage. This provides a view of all possible initiatives a particular concept is involved in and therefore an understanding of cross project or program dependencies.

VERSION COMPARE

Versions of concepts can be compared. The comparison will show the associations and concepts that have been created, updated or deleted for each version. A concept can be compared for two or more versions of the concept including the current version.

Concept compare is very different to a workspace compare. Workspace compare is about finding differences and gaps with a view to planning out work. Concept compare is about understanding what has changed and why on an individual component level.

COMMUNITIES

Community access to workspaces and concepts needs to be managed. Access control is critical.

Some workspaces may be created purely for protecting access privileges. For example, an organization may have an initiative to reduce head count for a particular part of the business in order to streamline it. However, this alternative should not be visible to all stakeholders. A community can be set up and assigned as a private community to work with this alternative workspace.

SUMMARY

The use of workspaces, baselines, and comparisons is essential for bridging the gap between the architecture of the enterprise and the architecture of a particular solution or initiative. As part of the architectural planning process we need to be able to manage parallel solutions whilst retaining the relationship with the enterprise continuum.

CHAPTER 14

PORTFOLIO MANAGEMENT

INTRODUCTION

Although this book is not directly about portfolio management, we thought we would lightly touch on the subject, as enterprise architecture can add significant value to the portfolio management process. This chapter focuses on the touch points of innovation management, enterprise architecture and portfolio management.

Any organization undertaking and IT related portfolio program of work such as application portfolio management or IT portfolio management would find this chapter useful.

OVERVIEW

Portfolio management is sometimes referred to as enterprise portfolio management and at other times project or program portfolio management and is owned in an organization by the portfolio management office.

Portfolio management provides portfolio managers with visibility into many programs and projects of work. Portfolio managers are also responsible for governance processes around the portfolio.

The goal of the portfolio management office (PMO) is to catalogue, quantify, cost manage and make best use of resources.

So, innovation management, enterprise architecture and portfolio management are very closely related activities but also very different.

Innovation managers, portfolio managers and enterprise architects often share the same views but their goals are very different.

For example, all are very interested in roadmaps. Innovation managers are interested in ideas, requirements and maybe product roadmaps.

Portfolio managers are primarily interested in initiatives, resource, projects and work package roadmaps.

Enterprise architects are interested in capability, process, application and technology roadmaps.

Ultimately the goal for innovation management is to provide a pipeline of ideas that are tied to campaigns that are driven by business goals.

Portfolio managers are looking at getting the best value out of initiatives and using resource and project spend wisely.

Enterprise architects are responsible for standardization, technology roadmaps, sometimes even business architecture and alignment with strategy.

All of these domains interact with each other at some level and often report into the chief innovation officer (CIO) within the organization who has ultimate responsibility for ensuring these parts of the jigsaw interact with one another.

Do we call it portfolio management, application portfolio management or enterprise portfolio management?

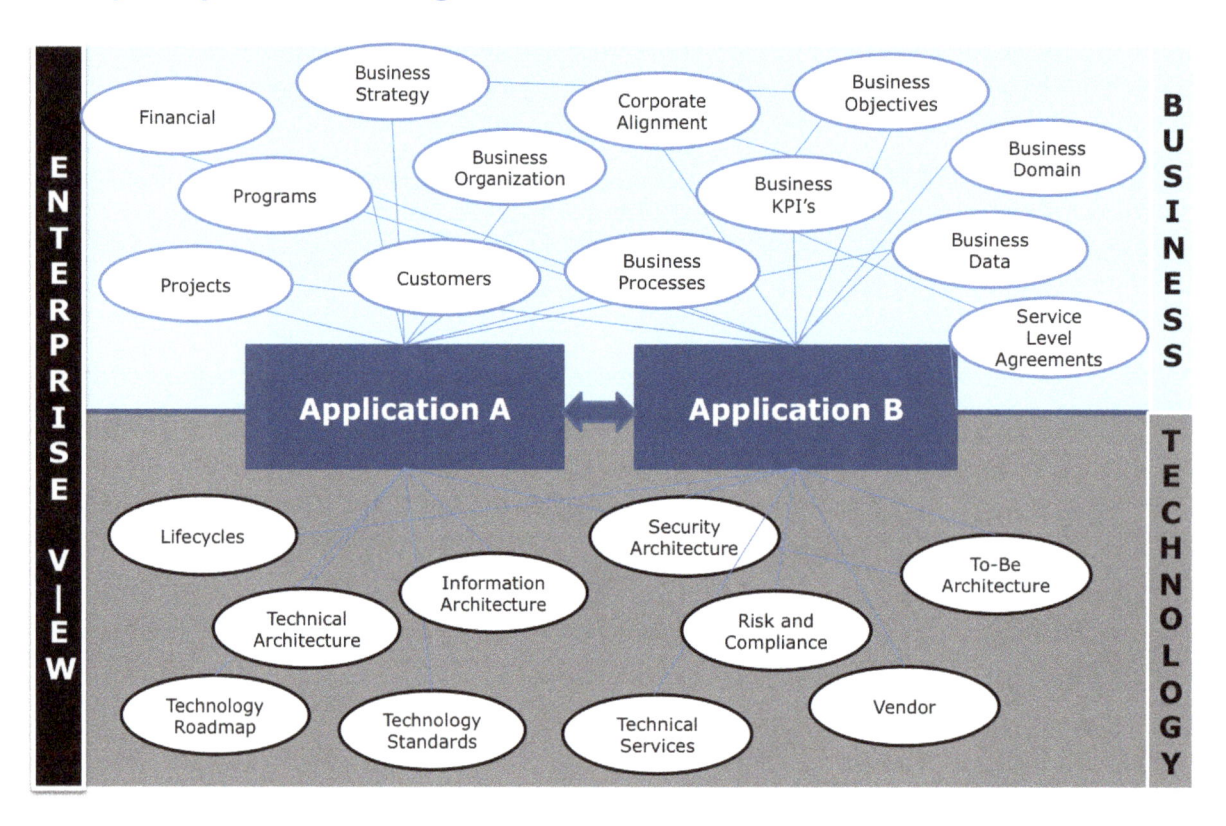

Figure 49: Applications within a portfolio management context

For example, Figure 49 illustrates that the domain of "Application Portfolio Management" is much broader than just applications.

On the top you can see just a small sample of the dozens of business meta-types that directly relate to the applications.

Other business context objects include:

Business functions, Business services, Capabilities, Financials, Business Data, etc....

On the lower half of this diagram you can see just a small sample of the dozens of technology objects directly related to the applications.

Other technology context objects include:

Interfaces, Master plans, Technology components, Application components, Security assets, etc.

Whatever view of your portfolio you're establishing, you will need a comprehensive view of both the business and technology relationships to your area of interest.

How many of these model meta-types can be aligned with enterprise architecture meta-models?

Most of the types in this diagram can relate to frameworks such as ArchiMate® and TOGAF®.

The underlying meta-model should not be siloed or fragmented.

MEASURING PORTFOLIO PERFORMANCE

Disparate data makes it difficult or impossible to get the real time information from the numerous sources needed to make sound investment decisions.

Portfolio management addresses these challenges by providing an integrated platform to effectively screen initial proposals, determine the best projects to invest in and ensure they are aligned with corporate strategic investments. It can link strategic objectives with the portfolio of initiatives so that investment decisions can be assessed in measurable ways. Portfolio management provides a framework for prioritizing and selecting these investments that have strong business case justification and analyzing them against available funding and resources. Portfolio performance should be assessed in real time to identify investment gaps and potential problems, like negative cash flow or lack of return on investment.

Following are some examples of typical portfolio management metrics that you may find useful.

NET PRESENT VALUE (NPV)

One of the Agile Enterprise Architecture product capabilities that lend itself to supporting Portfolio analysis is the support of Net Present Value (NPV). NPV is the discounting of cash values over time due to the reduction in expected rate of return in future years. This discount factor is the amount a subsequent future cash flow decreases over each period (commonly a year). In simple terms an expected benefit of £250,000 in 5 years time will be worth only a percentage of £250,000 in real terms once inflation has been applied.

Therefore when assessing either the costs or the benefits of an investment this discount rate should be applied.

Discounted Rate 0.07	Year 1 Cash 10000
Year 2 Cash 12500	Year 3 Cash 20000
Year 4 Cash 20000	Year 5 Cash 20000
Year 1 Benefit Cash 24500	Year 2 Benefit Cash 26500
Year 3 Benefit Cash	Year 4 Benefit Cash 20500
Year 5 Benefit Cash 15000	Business Assessment 88.89
Technical Assessment 37.5	Year 1 Benefit 22897.2
Year 2 Benefit 23146.13	Year 3 Benefit 19999.3
Year 4 Benefit 15639.35	Year 5 Benefit 10694.79
Year 1 Cost 9345.79	Year 2 Cost 10917.98
Year 3 Cost 16325.96	Year 4 Cost 15257.9
Year 5 Cost 14259.72	NPV Benefit 72377.47

Figure 50: Net present value calculation

If you take the NPV Cost and NPV Benefit from the Application Component in figure 50, then a net benefit can be seen over a five-year period. However, if you look at the actual costs and benefits in their $ value as of now then the calculation is different from a simple addition of each component. The difference is the discounted rate, in this case 7.5% per year. This approach ensures that the result to invest or not is not skewed by what seem high returns in later years and therefore provides a more accurate investment decision. The discount rate can be modified per concept as required.

The NPV Cost and Benefit attribute in the Concept are both examples of a Scorecard type attribute, which is discussed in more detail in another chapter of this book.

SUMMARY

Portfolio management is about making the right investment decisions and relies on information from many different sources including the architecture community and the project management office as part of a broad planning cycle. Enterprise Architecture is a key component of the activity to understand the wider architectural impact on an investment decisions especially when directly integrated into roadmapping.

Using Agile EA software allows this information to managed in such a way that makes it easy to provide the information required including applying techniques such as Net Present Value to provide a more precise calculation of future value streams.

CHAPTER 15

IDEAS TO DELIVERY

This topic looks at connecting ideas to delivery. We look at how innovation, enterprise architecture and successful project delivery needs to be intertwined and traceable.

OVERVIEW

Most organizations operate at a fast pace of change. Businesses are constantly evaluating market demands and enacting change to drive growth and develop a competitive edge. These market demands come from a broad number of sources, and include economic changes, market trends, regulations, technology improvements and resource management. Knowing where the demands originated, whether they are important and if they are worth acting on can be difficult.

In the past, managing ideation to the delivery of innovation has not been done or has been attempted in organizational silo's leading to disconnections. This in turn results in change not being implemented properly or a focus on the wrong type of change.

HOW DOES AN ORGANIZATION SUCCESSFULLY EMBRACE CHANGE?

Many companies start with campaigns and ideation. They run challenges and solicit ideas from within and outside of their walls. Ideas are then prioritized and evaluated. Sometimes prototypes are built and tested, but what happens next?

Many organisations turn to the blueprints or roadmaps generated by their EA, IT architectures and or business process architectures for answers. They evaluate how a new idea and its supporting technology, such as SOA or enterprise-resource planning (ERP), fits into the broader architecture. They manage their technology portfolio by looking at their IT infrastructure needs.

Organizations often form programme management boards to evaluate ideas, initiatives and their costs. In reality, these evaluations are based on lightweight business cases without the broader context. Organisations don't have a comprehensive understanding of what systems, processes and resources they have, what they are being used for, and how much they cost and the effects of regulations. Projects are delivered and viewed on a project-by-project basis without regard to the bigger picture. Enterprise, technology and process-related decisions are made within the flux of change and without access to the real knowledge contained within the organisation or in the market place. IT is often in the hot seat of this type of decision-making.

CHALLENGES OF IT PLANNING

IT planning takes place in reaction to and anticipation of these market demands and initiatives. There may be a need for a new CRM or accounting system, or new application for manufacturing or product development. While IT planning should be part of a broader enterprise architecture or market analysis, IT involvement in technology investments are often done close to the end of the strategic planning process and without proper access to enterprise or market data.

The following questions illustrate the competing demands found within the typical IT environment:

- **How can we manage the prioritization of business, architectural-and project-driven initiatives?** Stakeholders place a large number of both tactical and strategic requirements on IT. IT is required to offer different technology investment options, but is often constrained by a competition for resources.

- **How do we balance enterprise architecture's role with IT portfolio management?** An EA provides a high-level view of the risks and benefits of a project and the alignment to future goals. It can illustrate the project complexities and the impact of change. Future state architectures and transition plans can be used to define investment portfolio content. At the same time, portfolio management provides a detailed perspective of development and implementation. Balancing these often-competing viewpoints can be tricky.

- **How well are application lifecycles being managed?** Application management requires a product/service/asset view over time. Well-managed application lifecycles demand a process of continuous releases, especially when time to market is key. The higher-level view required by portfolio management provides a broader perspective of how all assets work together. Balancing application lifecycle demands against a broader portfolio framework can present an inherent conflict about priorities and a struggle for resources.

- **How do we manage the numerous and often conflicting governance requirements across the delivery process?** As many organizations move to small-team agile development, coordinating the various application development projects becomes more difficult. Managing the development process using waterfall methods can shorten schedules but can also increase the chance of errors and a disconnect with broader portfolio and enterprise goals.

- **How do we address different lifecycles and tribes in the organization?** Lifecycles such as innovation management, EA, business process management and solution delivery are all-necessary but are not harmonised across the enterprise. The connection among these lifecycles is important to the effective delivery of initiatives and understanding the impact of change.

The enterprise view, down through innovation management, portfolio management, application lifecycle management and agile development represent competing IT viewpoints that can come together using an ideas to delivery framework.

AGILE DEVELOPMENT AND DEVOPS

A key component of the drive from ideas to delivery is how strategic planning and the delivery of software are related or more directly the relevance of Agile Enterprise Architecture to DevOps.

DevOps is a term that has been around since the end of the last decade, originating from the Agile development movement and is a fusion of Development and Operations. In more practical terms it integrates developers and operations teams in order to improve collaboration and productivity by automating infrastructure, workflows and continuously measuring application performance.

The drivers behind the approach are the competing needs to incorporate new products into production whilst maintaining 99.9% uptime to customers in an agile manner.

Figure 51: Continuous delivery

To understand further the increase in complexity we need to look at how new features and functions need to be applied to our delivery of software. The world of mobile apps, middleware and cloud deployment has reduced release cycles to weeks not months with an emphasis on delivering incremental change. Previously a business release would be every few months with a series of modules and hopefully still relevant to the business goals.

The shorter continuous delivery lifecycle will help organizations:

▸ Achieve shorter releases by incremental delivery and delivering faster innovation

▸ Be more responsive to business needs by improved collaboration, better quality and more frequent releases.

▸ Manage the number of applications impacted by business release by allowing local variants for a global business and continuous delivery within releases

The DevOps approach achieves this by providing an environment that

▸ will minimize software delivery batch sizes to increase flexibility and enable continuous feedback as every team delivers features to production as they are completed.

▸ has the notion of projects are replaced by release trains which minimizes batch waiting time to reduce lead times and waste

- has a shift from central planning to decentralized execution with a pull philosophy thus minimizing batch transaction cost to improve efficiency

- makes DevOps economically feasible through test virtualization, build automation, and automated release management as we prioritize and sequence batches to maximize business value and select the right batches, sequence them in the right order, guide the implementation, track execution and make planning adjustments to maximize business value.

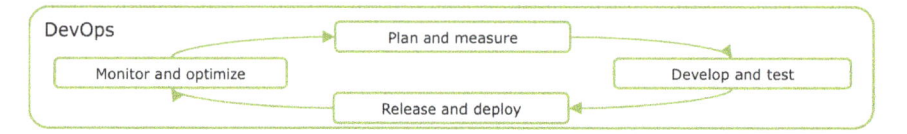

Figure 52: DevOps lifecycle

Thus far we have only looked at the delivery aspects, so how does this approach integrate with an Enterprise Architecture view?

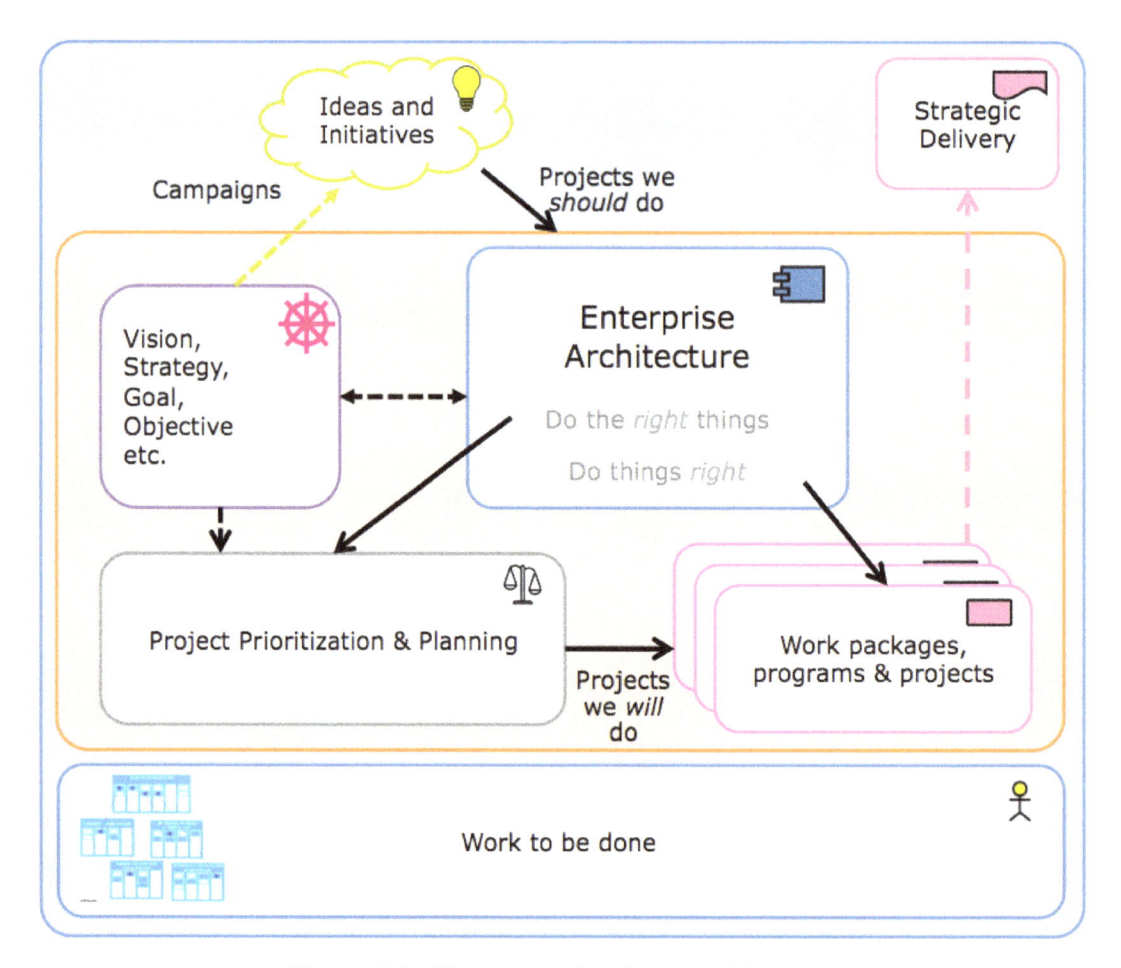

Figure 53: The strategic planning lifecycle

To understand this we need to look more closely at the Strategic Planning Lifecycle. Figure 53 shows how the strategic planning lifecycle supports an 'ideas to delivery' framework.

You can see here, the high level relationship between the strategy and goals of an organization and the projects that deliver the change to meet these goals. The Enterprise Architecture provides the model to govern the delivery of projects in line with these goals.

However we must ensure that any model that is built must be just enough EA to provide the right level of analysis and this has been discussed in previous sections of this book regarding the use of Kanban to drive change. The Agile EA model is then one that can both provide enough analysis to plan which projects should be undertaken and then to ensure full architectural governance over the delivery. The last part of this is achieved by connecting to the tools used in the Agile space.

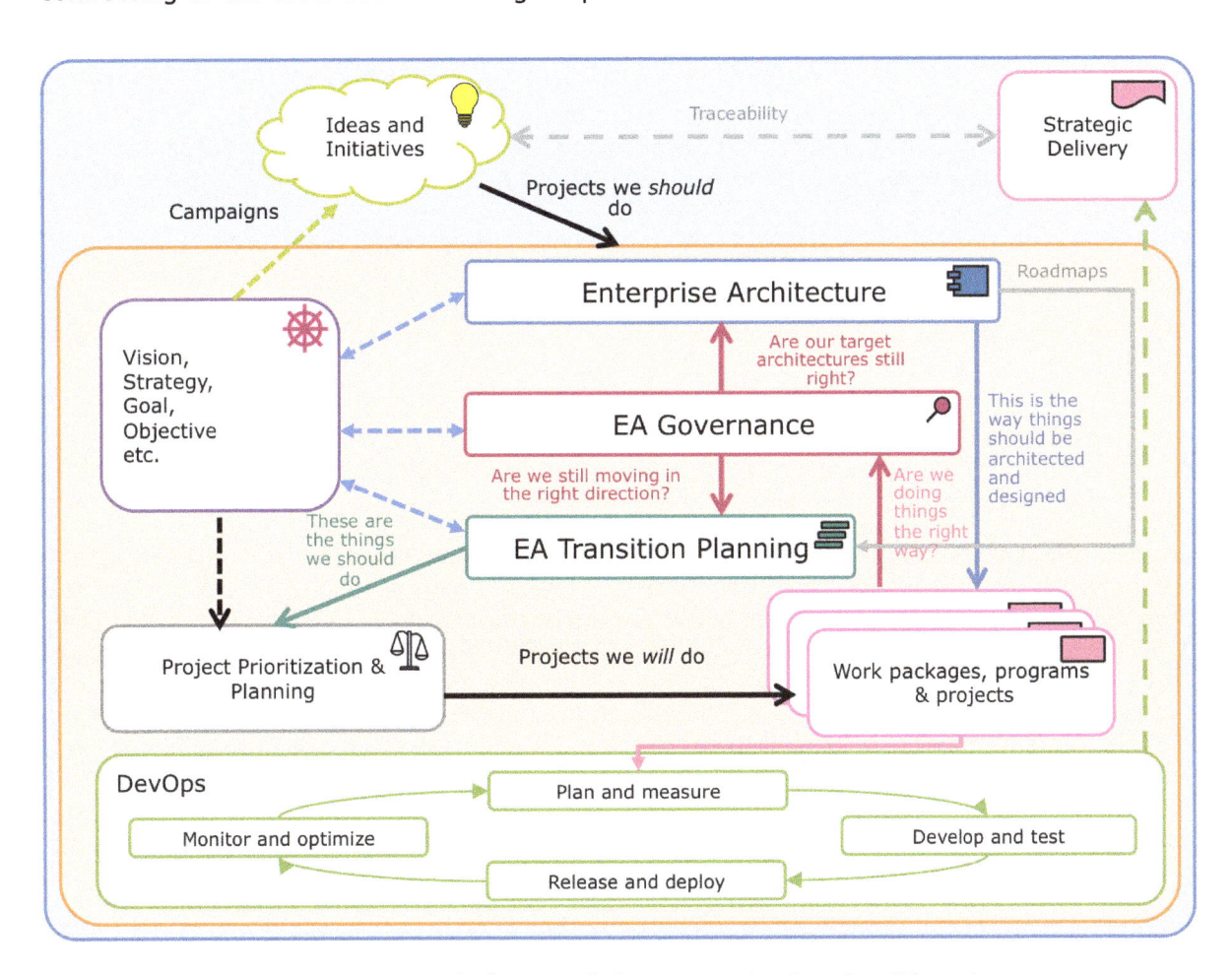

Figure 54: Detailed view of the strategic planning lifecycle

Page | 103

There are a number of tools that can be used within DevOps. Examples include Atlassian's JIRA, Rally Software, Microsoft's visual studio. Another example, is the IBM toolset, which uses open standards to link to other products within the overall lifecycle. This approach integrates the Agile Enterprise Architecture process with the Agile Development process and connects project delivery with effective governance of the project lifecycle and ensures that even if the software delivery process is agile the link to Goals and associated business needs are met.

To achieve this goal a number of internal processes must interoperate and this is a significant challenge, but one that can be met by building an internal centre of excellence and finding a solution by starting small and building a working environment.

THE STRATEGIC PLANNING LIFECYCLE SUMMARY

The organization begins by revisiting its corporate vision and strategy. What things will differentiate the organization from its competitors in five years? What value propositions will it offer customers to create that differentiation? The organization can create a series of campaigns or challenges to solicit new ideas and requirements for its vision and strategy.

The ideas and requirements are rationalized into a value proposition that can be examined in more detail.

The company can look at what resources it needs to have on both the business side and the IT side to deliver the capabilities needed to realize the value propositions. For example, a superior customer experience might demand better internet interactions and new applications, processes, and infrastructure on which to run. Once the needs are understood, they are compared to what the organization already has. The transition planning determines how the gaps will be addressed.

An enterprise architecture is a living thing with a lifecycle of its own. Figure 54 shows the ongoing EA processes. With the strategy and transition plan in place, EA execution begins. The transition plan provides input to project prioritization and planning since those projects aligned with the transition plan are typically prioritized over those that do not align. This determines which projects are funded and entered into, or continue to the DevOps stage. As the solutions are developed, enterprise architecture assets such as models, building blocks, rules, patterns, constraints and guidelines are used and followed. Where the standard assets aren't suitable for a project, exceptions are requested from the governance board. These exceptions are tracked carefully. Where assets are frequently the subject of exception requests, they must be examined to see if they really are suitable for the organization.

If we're not doing things the way we said we want done, then we must ask if our target architectures are still correct. This helps keep the EA current and useful.

Periodic updates to the organization's vision and strategy require a reassessment of the to-be state of the enterprise architecture. This typically results in another look at how the organization will differentiate itself in five years, what value propositions it will offer, the capabilities and resources needed, and so on. Then the transition plan is examined to see if it is still moving us in the right direction. If not, it is updated.

Figure 54, separates the organization's strategy and vision, the enterprise architecture lifecycle components and the solution development & delivery. Some argue that the strategy and vision are part of the EA while others argue against this. Both views are valid since they simply depend at how you look at the process. If the CEO's office is responsible for the vision and strategy and the reporting chain as responsible for its execution, then the separation of it from the EA makes sense. In practice, the top part of the reporting chain participates in the vision and strategy exercise and is encouraged to "own" it, at least from an execution perspective. In that case, it might be fair to consider it part of the EA. Or you can say it drives the EA. The categorization isn't as important as understanding how the vision and strategy interacts with the EA, or the rest of the EA, however you see it.

Note that the overall goal here is to have traceability from our ideas and initiatives, all the way through to strategic delivery. This comes with clear feedback from delivery assets to the ideas and requirements that they were initiated from.

CHAPTER 16

CREATING A BUSINESS CASE

So you've run a campaign and captured the relevant pieces of the architecture, you've got the key stakeholders and experts involved in evaluating your concepts and done some analysis of the architecture… what next?

You still need a solid business case that drives the delivery of your concepts.

One key objective of a business case is to persuade senior management to invest your organization's limited resources, money and time in your project (work package) rather than in a competing one. Another driver of a business case is to aid you in thinking through and making sense of what you've been coordinating.

OVERVIEW

The business case is a necessity in order to secure the resources, allocation of operating funds, or capital investment in any project, especially when applying a new capability, product or major upgrade or even buying up another company.

Every business case has a set of required inputs to make it successful. Here is an example list:

- Executive summary
- Work package or project name
- Business objectives and goals
- Market analysis
- Competitive analysis
- Capability or product description
- Target audience
- Sales and marketing plan
- Operational plan

- Complexity assessment

- Financial analysis, investment needs and break down and ROI

- Organizational areas affected (both internal and external), key stakeholders and dependencies

- Project or work package plan and schedule

- Required resources, including project management team, governance team, team members, funding

- Commitments required – project controls, reporting processes, deliverable schedule, financial budget schedule, roadmaps

A BUSINESS CASE SHOULD BE AGILE

It's a big list. But you'll soon start to notice if you look at the list carefully that you have most of this information already documented in your model.

If this were a list that you were working through without architecture, you'd struggle.

The intent of this list is good: business planning forces you to think through all the crucial elements of your delivery strategy.

However, writing a business case that takes weeks or months to put together and is not based on facts is a wasteful and costly exercise.

It becomes a document that is too big to read and too big to change. You need a more lean and systematic way to approach crafting delivery strategy and constructing business cases.

Something that:

- Is as collaborative as Google Docs to capture your vision, yet forces you to think through all the most important elements of any strategy.

- Can be easily shared with others to get their feedback in a format they'll actually read. People want in-person collaborations because of the fruitfulness of a natural conversation. So you need a tool that can easily enable those interactions.

- Provides a common language to discuss and debate strategy and architecture.

- Supports quick updates with live collaboration to the original vision, as assumptions are validated and new updates refine the strategy.

Essentially, you need something quick and efficient that will help you build your business case, whilst also getting traction with your internal stakeholders.

It is normal for business cases to go through a series of iterations of increasing depth throughout the innovation stage. A 'high-level' business case is often further refined in the lead-up to approval as assumptions, enterprise architecture assets and costs become clearer.

When you set out you may not know whether your business case will 'make sense', however by the time you finish you will have a detailed understanding of the business opportunities and risks for your project or work package.

However, at this stage, you are still being agile and developing "just enough" detail to make decisions.

Here is our 6 point flow for how to build an agile business case:

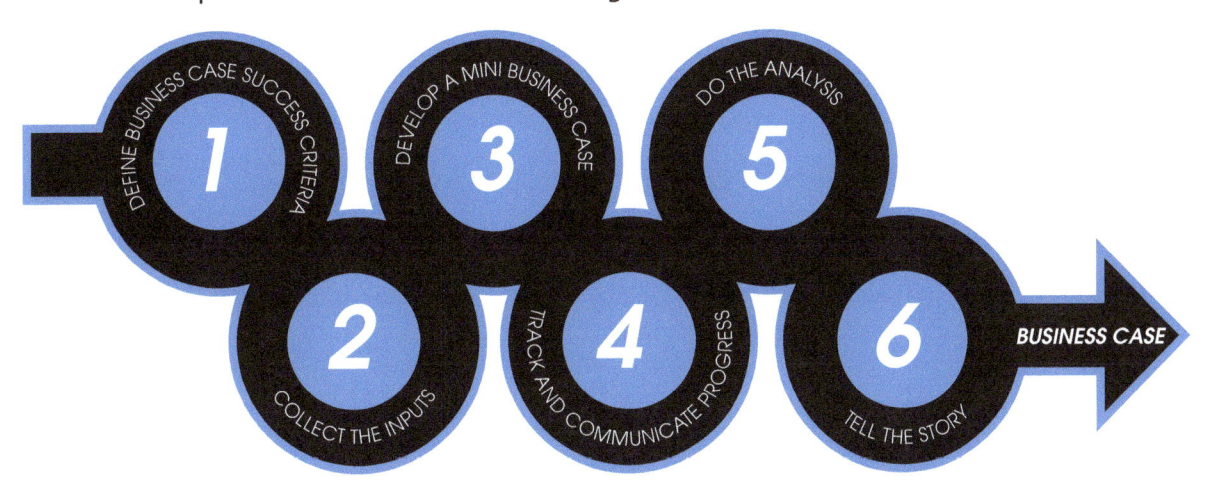

Figure 55: 6 point flow for business plan

1. DEFINE THE BUSINESS CASE SUCCESS CRITERIA

Many business cases evolved from one or more business ideas corroborated with some market research, subjective stakeholder feedback, and your gut feel or even a directive from a CxO.

Understanding how the people who judge your business case will make their decisions is vital. If you don't know what their criteria are, you'll be unsure as to which business benefits to aim at.

Your first step is to find a sponsor who cares about your success and who can provide guidance and support throughout the project and has the ability to drive change in your organization. Then you need to find out the timelines of what has to be done by when.

Next, look at the scope and constraints you have to work within and any existing processes you need to follow. Are there any steps that you don't need to do that will allow you to accelerate decision-making? For example, projects under $30,000 don't need executive approval.

The deliverable at this stage should be a plan that shows how you will develop and deliver the final business case. Create a mini-roadmap and model of the deliverables required using an ArchiMate or TOGAF model.

Start by looking towards your program management office (PMO) for feedback on successful business cases, what has worked in the past, what are the common mistakes and pitfalls that they always see?

To build the view you need to be able to answer the following questions:

- What roles need to be involved in the business case team to produce the business case, for example a program manager?
- Are there any experts that you need direct access to?
- Is there an existing company process or template to follow?
- Are there any key dates for which the business case must be ready e.g. a stage, gate or quarterly meeting?
- Who are the key decision makers and what's important to them?
- What deliverables need to be produced and by when?
- Are there any generally understood criteria that must be met, such as that all projects need to payback within two years and are aligned with the IT strategy?
- What format do stakeholders expect the business case to be delivered in? Presentation, spreadsheet, PDF or does it not matter?

1.1 UNDERSTAND YOUR VISION, GOALS AND DIRECTION

The first step is to write down your initial vision and start sharing it with stakeholders and partners for feedback. You can do this loosely or more formally using techniques such as the motivation extension in ArchiMate or the business motivation model (BMM).

1.2 IDENTIFY KEY RISKS AND MYSTERIES

When a new idea or set of requirements arrive, many people go straight ahead and talk with their Engineering or IT department to get level of effort (LOE) estimates. It may be more important though, to validate your target customer segment and their problems.

Initially, just about every aspect of your outline vision can be considered risky. The riskiest parts of your work package will depend on how well informed your vision may be. For example, if your organization has already done extensive market research, maybe your market segment and their concerns are not the riskiest components of your plan. Maybe it's the value proposition, your solution, or pricing model that may be the first things to corroborate.

You need to be able to quickly identify the riskiest parts that need to be tackled first so you can prioritize your work.

1.3 IDENTIFY KEY STAKEHOLDERS

The larger the organization you work in, the more stakeholders you're likely to have. It's important to identify who these folks are. Your enterprise architecture models will help you see who has the right competencies to help. If you're not sure who are your actual stakeholders are, then identify those most likely and track their involvement.

2. COLLECT INPUTS

The next stage is about assembling and gathering the detail you need to prepare the business case. This is the data you will use to build both your financial model and documented rationalization. Some of this will be understood and modelled but the rest of it may need to be assumed.

In a small business you may do much of this yourself; in larger enterprises there are lots of other people to collaborate with. This is a chance to gather verification of your business case from within and outside the organization to support the rationalization that is made. This evidence must convince people that any assumptions are representative, sound and objective.

2.1 SYSTEMATICALLY TEST YOUR PLAN AND START GATHERING DATA

Having identified your key risks and assumptions, and who you think are your key stakeholders, you're ready to start gathering qualitative and quantitative data.

For business strategy and market input you will need to talk to:

- People with access to market forecasts or research reports.

- Anyone with access to competitor info (or research this yourself).

- The strategy team (or whoever owns the business strategy). In a smaller organization, the directors or executive team will be able to help.

- Product marketing, to learn how your deliverables will be positioned against other products and propositions.

- Marketing, to learn about any other planned launches or promotions that might compete for resources. (This may provide you opportunities to align and grab some of their resources.)

- Business development, sales and channel managers.

For program and project input you will need to talk to:

- Solution architects to see what is happening downstream
- Enterprise architects to see the impact of your work package on their work
- Portfolio managers to see what projects are in the current portfolio that may impact this business case (is there anything in the pipeline you can piggy back upon?)
- IT costs and any related research and development funding required.

For sales and revenue input you will need to talk to:

- Relevant sales channels to get a view of the sales they believe they could make.
- Finance to get a view on metrics such as churn or ARPU (Average monthly Revenue Per User).
- Other successful business case owners to get their experience of take-up rates and also the assumptions they have used in their previous business cases.

For cost input you must talk to:

- Development and/or suppliers.
- Program management office to see potential costs of related resources.
- Marketing to understand the cost of marketing activities such as launching and promotions.
- Support functions to understand the cost of providing support e.g. any recruitment required, any necessary IT system updates.

3. DEVELOP A MINI BUSINESS CASE

As early as possible, you need to produce a quick assessment on the business potential of the outcome of your work package to determine whether the idea is worth pursuing from a financial perspective.

This is particularly relevant if your organization, as part of its corporate strategy, has set minimum financial criteria on the types of business opportunities it's willing to fund, and at what level it considers an investment a capital expense (Capex) vs. an operational expense (Opex)

This makes sense to do once you have some preliminary data on your target customer, specifically, the addressable market size and share you think you can capture; the viability of your pricing strategy and revenue model; and at least high-level cost estimates. The numbers may be approximations, but they should be substantiated enough in reality to not be just guesstimates. Your data collecting activities from earlier should serve to inform this analysis.

An example mini business case outline structure follows:

1. Understanding Resistance
   - What is the customer situation?
   - What is the customer need?
   - What is the customer resistance?

2. Our idea
   - Description of the target audience
   - Description of the new idea
   - Is the deliverable new to us, new to the market, new to the world?
   - Are we targeting an existing or new market?

3. This is the benefit for the customer
   - Why will the customer choose this idea?
   - What makes us unique?
   - Who are our main competitors (if any)?
   - What's our positioning?
   - What are our strengths and weaknesses?

4. We can produce, make or build it
   - What is the viability of our deliverable?
   - Who are the potential partners for co-creation?
   - What are the next steps in the development process?
   - Have we prototyped our concept?
   - Do we know the impact of our concept on the organization/IT infrastructure?

5. This is what our company becomes/gets
   - Potential turnover
   - Potential margin and profits
   - On-going costs for development and maintenance

- Other related benefits this work provides (cultural, social, new products/services)

6. How we will continue in this way

- Why proceed?

- What are the risks?

- Next steps: prototype/team-planning costs

This quick analysis is especially useful in early discussions with CFOs, the finance department, and business executives. It can also help with strategic prioritization discussions, and may be useful if your organization follows agile estimation techniques such as t-shirt sizing, Fibonacci sequence or powers of 2.

If you have many requirements or features that need prioritizing as part of a mini business case, it is worth looking at analytical hierarchy process (AHP). This will allow you to produce a summarized list of the priorities for your business case.

4. TRACK AND COMMUNICATE PROGRESS

The business case needs supporters both inside and outside the organization. You need to involve these people as collaborators and its useful if they are upstream, downstream and parallel to you in the business.

This helps you generate and sustain momentum for your work and enables them to feel part of the process. Your initiative gains further supporters and buy in.

The formation community empowers others to communicate about your initiative.

Here is where you can communicate using collaboration tools such as the Corso Strategic Planning Platform (SPP) that will enable stakeholders to be part of communities and are thereby part of your strategy and mission.

It definitely beats having to maintain presentation slides and emails.

As you validate your assumptions and de-risk your strategy, you can keep the community abreast of what's happening. What's more, you're using formal techniques to describe the goals and strategy so they are consistent across other business cases ensuring they can be measured against each other.

Next, you need to produce the formal business case presentation

As you continue to refine your deliverable and strategy through the activities above, you will be in a position to start writing an official business case, if such a formal document is really needed in your organization.

The difference now is that you will have not only validated inputs via data to ground your business case (like your companies financial figures), but also garnered the necessary "pre-support" to make a decision more of a formality.

5. DO THE ANALYSIS

During the analysis stage you study the inputs you've now gathered to build a detailed model of your product and your development project.

If you don't have a tool that will allow you to model various scenarios and understand sensitivity analysis, you will need a spreadsheet. A typical business case financial model is broken down into a section on assumptions, a section on income (revenue), a section on costs and then a section that calculates the project value in terms of profit or payback.

You will find the following financial measures useful in any business case:

Net Present Value (NPV)
Measures the excess or shortfall of cash flows, in present terms, once financing charges are met. If NPV is greater than 0 the project may be accepted; if the NPV is less than 0 then the project should be rejected.

Internal Rate of Return (IRR)
A rate of return used in capital budgeting to measure and compare the profitability of investments. It is defined as the annualised effective compound return rate

Return On Investment (ROI)
A measure of cash generated or lost due to the investment

Pay Back Period (PBR)   The period of time required for the return on an investment to 'repay' the sum of the original investment (Wikipedia 2011)

Total Cost of Ownership (TCO)
The total value of acquisition and operating costs

	2015	2016	2017	2018	2019	Total
Discount rate	5%					
Cash invested	-400,000					
Revenue	100,000	100,000	100,000	100,000	100,000	500,000
Net cash	-300,000	100,000	100,000	100,000	100,000	
Cash flow	-200,000	-100,000	0	100,000	200,000	
PV	-285,714	90,703	86,384	82,270	78,353	
IRR	13%					
P&R (years)	3	2017				
NPV	51,995					
ROI	25%					

The previous table contains a simple example of a financial analysis in a business case that requires a once off investment of 400,000 and generates revenue of 500,000 over 5 years.

We can see from this that the ROI is 25%

ROI is nothing more than a simple calculation using the following formula:

ROI = Gains − Investment Costs / Investment Costs = 500,000 − 400,000 / 400,000 = 25%

IRR is the internal rate of return. The IRR is a good way of judging different investments. First of all, the IRR should be higher than the cost of funds.

If it costs you 8% to borrow money, then an IRR of only 6% is not good enough!

IRR is also useful when investments are quite different.

Maybe the amounts involved are quite different or maybe one has high costs at the start, and another has many small costs over time.

The financials are only part of the business case but are certainly the first port of call for anybody analysing the business case. You should treat the business case as a deliverable of your work package. There will be a cost for putting together the business case itself.

6. TELL THE STORY

The final stage of the business case process is to present or deliver the business case to the appropriate decision maker(s), whether this is an investment board or an individual.

No-one can predict the outcome with certainty, so your success rests on the credibility of the case you make – the suppositions you use, the proof you can gather, the support you line-up, the thoroughness of your analysis and last but not least, your personal integrity.

This may be through a presentation where you have the chance to explain your business case in detail or through the delivery of a document for review.

If you're not comfortable presenting, that's ok. Why not find a stakeholder in a community that you feel can help add weight to your case?

The challenge is to keep the story clear, objective and plausible. If a decision maker doesn't understand it, they are unlikely to believe it and will find holes in your business case.

If you can, it is often worth petitioning decision makers before an approval process to see if they are on-board, if they have any concerns and if they judge that input from their areas has been satisfactorily characterised. Hopefully, you'll have built up a good rapport in step 4 with your communities.

Primarily, a business case is a tool to sell your investment work package and outcomes (eg. your new product, suggestion) to the business.

SUMMARY

There are always many ways to spend an organization's money so most businesses have a standard process to produce business cases.

The process normally includes the ability to compare one business case against another and to make it easy to say 'yes' to the right ones and 'no' to the wrong ones. Often these decisions are owned and governed by the program management office (PMO).

A good business case should provide you with a significant advantage in the context of other projects. Following the six steps should ensure that a rigorous assessment of a new work package has been completed and has provided a level of investigation and analysis that should ensure (as far as is possible) the outcome is a success.

In an perfect world, the financial model, its assumptions become a tool that can be used to manage the work package through it's life time.

CHAPTER 17

CENTRE OF EXCELLENCE

The Centre of Excellence (CoE) is a broad set of activities, delivered alongside tooling to embed the use of software tools to support the Governance of future IT project design. The CoE helps achieve a business as usual status use of innovation management and enterprise architecture models.

To achieve this goal a series of activities must take place to allow the transition from a set of reactive data capture activities to a proactive use of the tool in Governing future IT development and being a trusted component of the delivery lifecycle.

The following section outlines the activities, responsibilities and skills required to make the Centre of Excellence (CoE) a reality.

OVERVIEW

The following is a summary of the responsibilities and tasks of the CoE grouped by skill-set. The CoE is in place to create a point of access to support the embedding of Agile Enterprise Architecture tooling. It is a combination of people, training collateral, discussion groups and support centre to allow the wider user group to better use the tools. The CoE will be central to the transition of the product from one of data capture to one of pro-actively supporting the design process.

It is also best practice to start referring to the model rather than the tool, thus the benefit to an organisation is not the tool but the effective use of the data within it and therefore it is the model that must be kept up to date not the tool. By referring to the model there is generally better buy in from the users as inherently people equate learning how to use tools, even a simplified agile tool, with delay and they fail to see the benefit of the what an up to date model can bring. The CoE should provide all the base materials for new users to learn how to use the tool in the context of how to use the model.

ADMINISTRATION

The CoE is responsible for the administration of the software and user access, this is both a technical and business role. Firstly as an administrator to technically maintain the users, contributors and reviewers but also to understand the business needs of the platform to maintain the right mix of license types.

It is essential to align the use of communities on the platform with the structure of the users and so the CoE builds the community structure within the product to represent the business needs of either an Innovation management or Agile Enterprise Architecture initiative.

MODELING

The CoE oversees any modeling exercise and so is responsible for the data within the repository and its structure. This includes management of the meta-model, workspaces and ensuring data quality across the models.

The CoE should be involved early in the data collection process and so the initial modeling exercise including importing of data from existing sources and resolving issues of quality and consistency is an important aspect. However the maintaining data quality is something that must be addressed at all times.

The key areas of modeling responsibility can be broken down to the following:

- Importing data from different sources and building the initial models.
- Ensure the integrity of the models including reviewing and removing obsolete definitions and diagrams
- Model Quality – especially do the models correspond to the methodology and approach of the business
- Data Quality – Is the data complete or correct?
- Data Consistency – Is there duplicate data? Does a particular data item need resolution if defined in different ways by different parts of the organization.
- Working with subject matter experts to update the model.

TECHNICAL

The CoE role also oversees the technical aspects of the products and so there should be a deep knowledge of the functionality available and how it can be best deployed by the users. The CoE should look to attain a help desk level of support for the tooling, which would include the following:

- Managing Concepts and Associations
- Pairwise Comparison
- Kanban
- Charts and Pivot Tables

- Roadmaps
- Working with Diagrams

It is also important to know what maybe in the vendor feature pipeline and to get an early understanding of how new functionality can help the users.

MENTOR AND TRAINING

To ensure adoption of any software product there needs to be documentation. However, although software such as Corso's is easy to adopt, effective documentation involves real world examples with data that a user readily understands and this is why we need to develop exemplar models that walk through the end-to-end modeling process.

The exemplar models must reflect a specific worked example that can be readily understood by the organization, including all expected meta-type and association examples but not too detailed. The same model can then be presented to different audiences as required in a kick off workshop. The following is an example agenda:

- Overview of the model and the process (5-10 minutes)
- Demonstration of the product capabilities (45 Minutes)
- New User start up - a document based walkthrough of the model incorporating how it can be manipulated in Corso Agile Enterprise Architecture, this can double up as training materials and User Guides (3 hours)
- Training materials with step by step guide to product usage

The CoE will build the above materials and should distribute them through a shared portal with other supporting materials such as white papers and blogs to build an on-line community. The sharing of relevant information in a single location fosters the sense of community and is proven to improve the uptake of the software.

A combination of a physical CoE and an on-line portal ensure that there will be a place for current and potential users to go and find information as and when they need it.

COORDINATION

As Innovation Management or AgileEA implementations become more mature they must also evolve. It is the CoE's responsibility to manage this evolution in a structured manner. The CoE must:

- Manage user requirements New requirements will always come from users. These could be modified attributes, relationships, reports, Kanban, charts or Pivot Tables. Care must be taken to manage the changes strategically to keep the environment agile.

- **Agile EA must be embedded within the wider change process** The CoE must ensure that the Agile EA tool be embedded in the design process and PMO otherwise our models will remain isolated. The Roadmapping capability and use of Communities within a tool is key to supporting this.

- **Coordinate with Solution Architects to transition into using the tool for design.** As part of incorporating the tools into the wider design phase Solution Architects should be involved. The use of the workspace and Kanban capability to manage change around a particular context is key to supporting this.

- **Work with** the vendor to understand how to phase these changes in and develop an internal roadmap for the tool roll out.

SELLING

One last key but often-overlooked responsibility of the CoE is to internally evangelise the use of the tools and approach with current and future stakeholders. It is essential to build the CoE 'brand' within your organization.

Visibility will need to be earned by a strategic approach to getting the message across to the multiple stakeholders involved in the Innovation or Agile EA process. This can sometimes be a long process but with the right level of management commitment, a range of highly relevant materials and the enthusiasm to push things forward the CoE can flourish and provide a platform for a successful product implementation that provides tangible benefit.

The individuals responsible for the CoE should have multiple skills. These skills must include technical knowledge to understand the models themselves and to build technical teaching documents but there should also be an element of sales and project management.

EXAMPLE OF RETURN ON INVESTMENT

The following started out as an exercise in understanding the value of building Architecture models and embedding these within the IT delivery process at a Dutch bank for a Portfolio Management project. The following 5 measures were highlighted as potential cost savings, importantly each saving was small (2-5%) but when multiplied by the overall IT spend provided a strong case for the investment of resources and tools to build and maintain the model.

IMPROVING THE ARCHITECTURE PROCESS

- Using a central, repository based, multi-user Enterprise Architecture modeling solution (Agile Enterprise Architecture) enables clearer and controlled collaboration between different teams. This has shown improved project delivery times, with the added benefit of improved quality of information. Note the improvements and benefits will increase over time as 'the organization' becomes familiar with the new process and discipline.

- This is especially useful at the beginning of each project during the discovery of information stage.

- Direct benefit for 'the organization' is a 5% improvement on the costs of the architectural function in Design Authorities costs.

PROJECT GOVERNANCE

- In addition to using Enterprise Architecture to govern the delivery of projects within 'the organization', there are additional benefits from the software delivery function working together with the Project Management Office in reusing across program architecture to derive shared technologies, solutions and processes across future projects.

- Benefit for 'the organization' is a 5% direct saving in investments made through the ability of making consistent technology buying decisions across total project spend across each 'the organization' business vertical/unit

MITIGATING RISK OF POST PROJECT REWORK

- One of the common failings of project-by-project delivery is delivering in isolation and then having to rework changes.

- Having a single Enterprise Architecture modeling tooling solution could deliver 3-5% improvement on project overspend by getting the full impact of changes understood prior to project initiation. In addition, money set aside to mitigate the risk of poor project delivery can be reassigned to money generating activities.

REMOVING COST FROM THE IT LANDSCAPE

- The core deliverables of a Portfolio Management project are still relevant over and above the broad cost savings from deploying an Agile Enterprise Architecture approach.

- With the ability of removing cost from the IT Landscape via a well developed and delivered Enterprise Architecture program, as a by-process of better understanding the functionality of the IT Applications and associated annual Maintenance, 'the organization' will be able to remove overlapping applications, retire legacy systems, reduce maintenance and help implement a more service driven environment.

- Anticipated cost reductions across 'the organization 'would be 10% savings year in year IT support/maintenance costs.

RETENTION OF INFORMATION

- Individuals who leave 'the organization 'or move' to other roles take their knowledge with them which reduces the quality of the information. Maintaining a central repository of agreed and qualified artefacts will keep some of this information in the public domain and can be reused when delivering future projects.

- There is a potential 5% increase in the cost of architecture function.

CHAPTER 17

FINAL SUMMARY

This book has covered the need for strategic planning within an IT context.

Many of the concepts and ideas in this book are not new but have been brought together to provide a set of techniques that can help any organization address the issue of change management within the context of innovation and IT delivery.

The techniques have been integrated into the Corso Strategic Planning Platform (SPP), which provides many of the capabilities described in the book.

STRATEGIC PLANNING PLATFORM

In most organizations, Enterprise Architecture (EA), IT and business/operations have their own technology and planning process. No area is equipped to offer an integrated platform that takes into account the different viewpoints needed for strategic IT decisions. Often, this is due to both cultural and technological integration issues. Social media tools provide a platform to start the process with ideas, but must interface to other technologies that can be integrated across multiple platforms. For example, an EA offers a framework for high-level, big picture perspectives, but cannot capture the business view where opinion, revenue, risk appetite, competition and sales goals are the vocabulary.

A strategic planning platform brings together all areas of the organization—including innovation management, portfolio management, PMO, IT and business—to facilitate decision-making. It helps teams analyze and prioritize ideas, feed them into the EA, then translate the business case to projects that can be approved by the PMO and implemented by IT.

A strategic planning platform consists of a process, a method and a framework. It identifies the landscape of systems being used and provides a roadmap for change. It brings together the three internal perspectives that drive change: Markets (business), Capability (enterprise architecture) and Delivery (IT). It helps an organization use existing technology to fill the gaps or determine the need and requirements for new technologies. It can determine the impact of any new idea, small or large, on the organization and its systems. It offers a way to systematically manage change while embracing an organization's many stakeholders. It extends beyond the EA to provide one integrated platform for everyone to understand how new ideas fit into the corporate strategy. A strategic planning platform puts the action into EA and provides a platform for cultural change.

A FEDERATED VIEW OF DATA

One of the challenges that all organizations face is easily sharing information. The major benefit of this type of platform is its ability to embrace both new and old technologies and facilitate smart decisions and plans for change. Sharing and linking information is no longer a hurdle to strategic planning.

A strategic planning platform also works in cloud environments and as SaaS (software as a service), where software applications are hosted and managed by a vendor or service provider. Socialization and harvesting are done in harmony with the cloud. Information can be collected at any time and placed inside or outside firewall.

Many organizations are working in a federated and globally distributed team. Mobility is key in planning and accessing and communicating with other stakeholder at anytime and anywhere is key to success.

By adopting a strategic planning framework, organizations can capture and analyse new ideas, then translate those with merit into actionable plans for business and IT. Anyone can freely ask questions about the project. Has the idea already been rejected? Is it already being implemented somewhere in the organization? Does it have a solid business case justifying it? Do we have funding to make it happen?

All of the techniques described in this book require collaboration and the ability to interact with model data regardless of device or location.

A range of new platforms supporting strategic planning is now becoming available including the strategic planning platform from Corso which embodies both an Agile EA and Innovation Management solution.

CUSTOMIZATION IS IMPORTANT

Each organization has unique challenges and requirements for planning. Some organization have processes for project sign off that involve many stakeholders, whilst others are very loose. Some companies are financially driven, some are 'not for profit', for some research is key. Customization of a process and views should always take place. The work products in this book are a starting point for you to get ideas from and to start moving your innovation management and/or enterprise architecture practice forward.

Its rare to see an organization that adopts a framework and views such as ArchiMate "out of the box". Time should be taken to configure a planning approach that all stakeholders see 'adds value' to their daily roles and ultimately provides a benefit to the company.

APPENDIX A

ANALYTICAL HIERARCHY PROCESS (AHP) EXAMPLE

USING AHP

In the following examples, it is not unusual to carry out decision-making involving dozens or even hundreds of concepts. The math behind AHP can be done by hand or with a spreadsheet but to manage the on-going AHP it is highly recommended to use a tool, especially where teams/communities are geographically dispersed.

The procedure for using the AHP is summarized as:

1. Model the problem as a hierarchy containing the decision goal, the alternatives for reaching it, and the criteria for evaluating the alternatives.

2. Establish priorities among the elements of the hierarchy by making a series of judgments based on pairwise comparisons of the elements. For example, when comparing application components within an application portfolio rationalization exercise, the architects might say they prefer cost reduction to new capability and new capability over software as a service (SaaS).

3. Synthesize these judgments to yield a set of overall priorities for the hierarchy. This would combine the architects' judgments about cost, capability and SaaS for applications A, B, C, and D into overall priorities for each application.

4. Check the consistency of the judgments.

5. Come to a final decision based on the results of this process

These steps are more fully described below.

MODEL THE PROBLEM AS A HIERARCHY

The first step in the AHP is to model the problem as a *hierarchy*. In doing this, participants break down and investigate aspects of the problem at levels from general to detailed, then express it in the decomposed way that the AHP needs. As they work to build the hierarchy, they increase their understanding of the problem, of its context, and of each other's thoughts and feelings about both.

A hierarchy is a decomposition style of ranking and organizing concepts, where each concept of the system, except for the top one, is subordinate to one or more other concepts.

Concepts in hierarchies must be associated to each other in the underlying model and in an order that expresses the hierarchy.

IM and EA concepts are often structure as hierarchies. Examples include Goal, Actor, Role and Campaign, Goal, Idea

Architects often break down concepts into further levels of detail.

Imagine a hierarchy that a data architect uses while discovering data entities. They separately consider the subject areas (including subject area associations), the data entities (including associations and cardinality) and attributes (including keys and data types) until they've covered the entire domain they're investigating. Advanced architects continue breaking down the data all the way to individual elements and sometimes-physical mappings. In the end, the data architects understand the enterprise data model and a considerable number of its details.

By working hierarchically, they've gained a comprehensive understanding of enterprise data.

Similarly, when we approach a complex decision problem, we can use a hierarchy to integrate large amounts of information into our understanding of the situation. As we build this information structure, we form a better and better picture of the problem as a whole.

HIERARCHIES IN THE AHP

An AHP hierarchy is a structured means of modeling the decision at hand. It consists of an overall *goal*; a group of *alternatives* for reaching the goal, and *criteria* that relate the alternatives to the goal.

There are published descriptions of AHP applications that include diagrams and descriptions of their hierarchies; some simple ones are shown throughout this chapter.

The design of any AHP hierarchy will depend not only on the nature of the problem at hand, but also on the knowledge, judgments, values, opinions, needs, wants, etc. of the participants in the decision-making process. Constructing a hierarchy typically involves significant discussion, research, and discovery by those involved.

To better understand AHP hierarchies, consider a decision problem with a goal to be achieved, four alternative ways of reaching the goal, and three criteria against which the alternatives need to be measured.

Such a hierarchy can be visualized as a diagram like the one immediately below, with the goal at the top, the four alternatives at the bottom, and the three criteria in between.

The goal is the parent of the three criteria, and the three criteria are children of the goal.

Each criterion is a parent of the four Alternatives. Note that there are only four Alternatives, but in the diagram, each of them is repeated under each of its parents.

In Figure 56, there are four Alternatives for reaching the Goal, and three Criteria to be used in deciding among them.

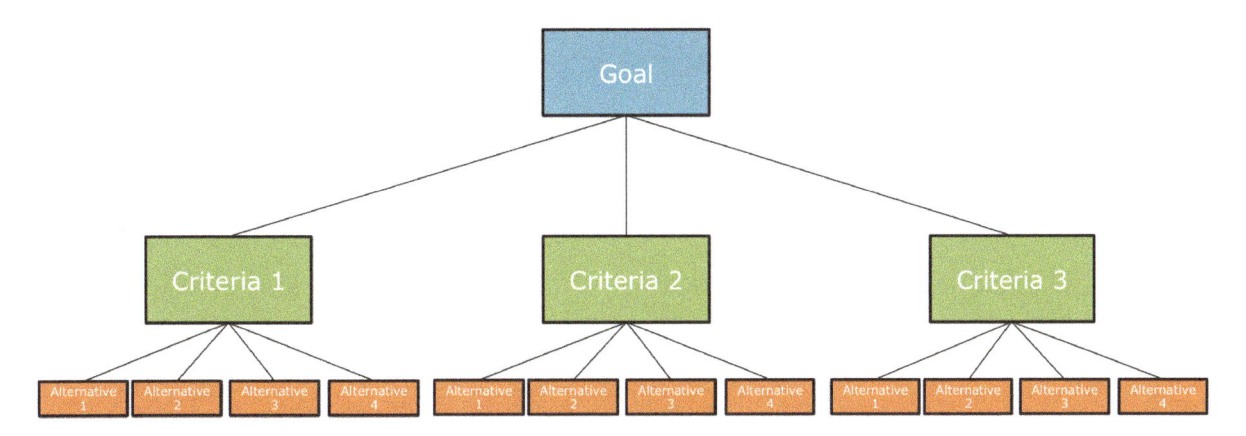

Figure 56: a simple AHP hierarchy

Alternatively, the hierarchy could be drawn as in Figure 57.

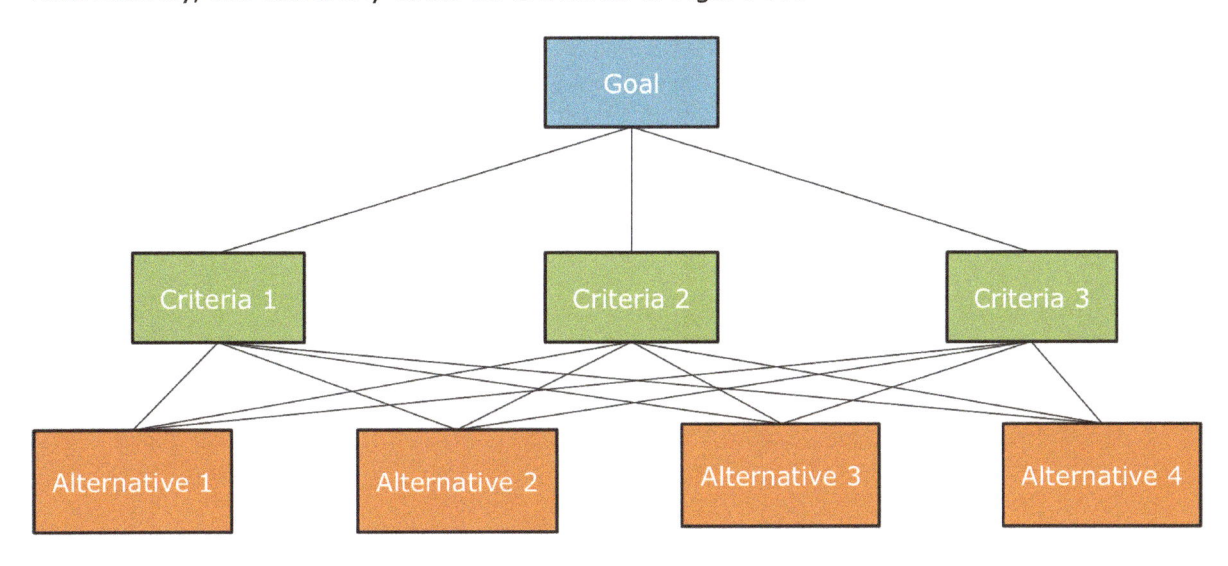

Figure 57: Alternative AHP representation

EVALUATE THE HIERARCHY

Once the hierarchy has been constructed, the participants analyze it through a series of *pairwise comparisons* that derive numerical priorities for each of the concepts. The criteria are pairwise compared against the goal for importance. The alternatives are pairwise compared against each of the criteria for choice. The comparisons are processed mathematically, and *priorities* are derived for each node.

Consider the "Reduce customer facing operational costs" example shown by Figure 58. An important task of the decision makers is to determine the weight to be given each criterion in reducing costs for customer facing operations. Another important task is to determine the weight to be given to each alternative with regard to each of the criteria. The AHP not only lets them do that, but it lets them put a meaningful and objective numerical value on each of the three criteria.

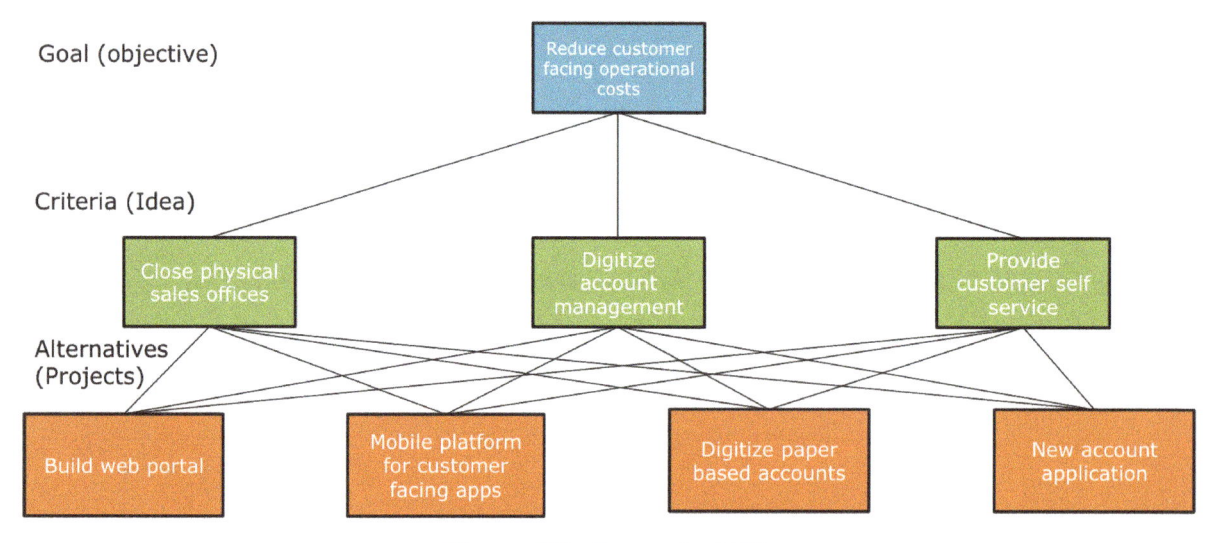

Figure 58: Example AHP

You will also notice in Figure 58 that we've applied particular concepts to the goal, criteria and alternative. Now you can see how this relates the underlying model and meta-model that we've covered in other chapters.

ESTABLISH PRIORITIES

This section explains priorities, shows how they are established, and provides a simple example.

Priorities are numbers associated with the concepts of an AHP hierarchy. They represent the relative weights of the concepts in any group with its siblings. Sibling concepts are concepts that share the same parent concept in the hierarchy.

Depending on the problem at hand, "weight" can refer to importance, or preference, or likelihood, or the decision makers are considering.

Priorities are distributed over a hierarchy according to its architecture, and their values depend on the information entered by users of the AHP. Priorities of the Goal, the Criteria, and the Alternatives are intimately related, but need to be considered separately.

By definition, the priority of the Goal is 1.000. The priorities of the alternatives always add up to 1.000, and the criteria priorities also add to 1.000. All this is illustrated by the priorities in Figure 59.

Observe that the priorities on each level of the example—the goal, the criteria, and the alternatives—all add up to 1 or any other given whole amount e.g. 100

The priorities shown are those that exist before any information has been entered about weights of the criteria or alternatives, so the priorities within each level are all equal. They are called the hierarchy's *default priorities*.

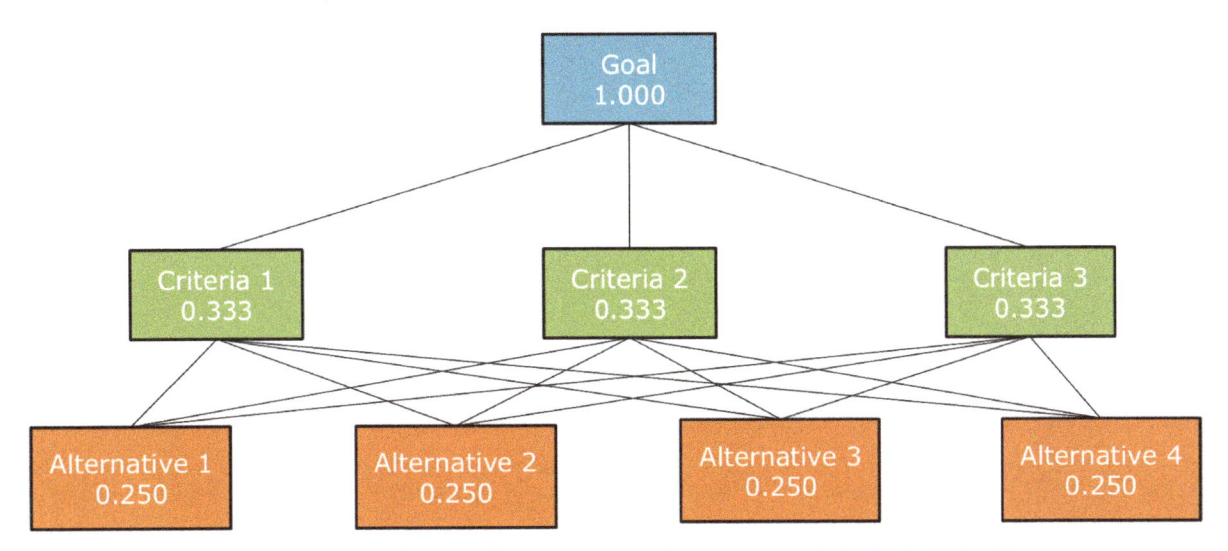

Figure 59: Simple AHP hierarchy with associated default priorities

So far, we have looked only at default priorities. As the Analytical Hierarchy Process moves forward, the priorities will change from their default values as the decision makers input information about the importance of the various concepts. They do this by making a series of pairwise comparisons.

PAIRWISE COMPARISONS

For each level in the hierarchy, we compare each concept against the other.

So for our goal, we compare its child concepts one against another.

In this example it would be Criteria 1 v Criteria 2, Criteria 1 v Criteria 3 and Criteria 2 v Criteria 3.

We can also represent this in a matrix:

	Criteria 1	Criteria 2	Criteria 3
Criteria 1			
Criteria 2			
Criteria 3			

The comparisons can be made in any order and the comparison at criteria or alternative level can be done in any sequence too.

Each member of a community can make a comparison and decide which of a pair is weaker.

The following scale can be used to show the intensity of the importance of one concept over another.

The fundamental scale for pairwise comparisons		
Importance	Name	Description
1	Equal importance	Two concepts contribute equally to the objective
3	Moderate importance	Experience and judgment moderately favour one concept over another
5	Strong importance	Experience and judgment strongly favour one concept over another
7	Very strong importance	Once concept is very strongly favoured one concept over another
9	Extreme importance	The evidence for one concept being favorable over another is of the highest affirmation.

PAIRWISE EXAMPLE

Using our "Reduce customer facing operational costs" example:

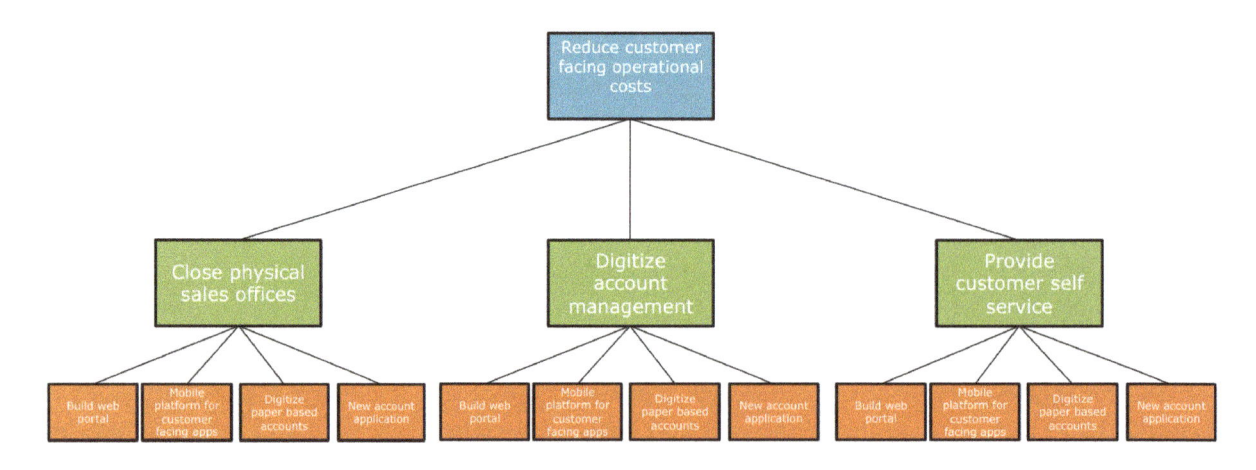

Figure 60: Pairwise example

We can compare each of our criteria in the context of the overall goal to reduce our customer facing operational costs, using the scale for pairwise comparisons:

Close physical sales offices	9	Digitize account management	1	Our biggest financial cost is operating sales offices so that outweighs digitizing account management.
Close physical sales offices	5	Provide customer self service	1	Again, our biggest financial outlay is sales offices but we do need to provide a way for customers to self serve.
Digitize account management	1	Provide customer self service	3	We do not necessarily have to digitize account management to achieve costs, so we can moderately favour providing self service

We can now transfer these weights into the matrix. This method is unique to AHP. For each pairwise comparison, the weights are assigned to the matrix. Reading each pair, row by row in the table, does this. And next placing the highest number in the cell intersection that corresponds to the name of the concept with the highest number and the column of the lowest ranked concept for that pair. The reciprocal of that number is placed into the corresponding cell of the column that represents the pair of concepts.

	Close physical sales offices	Digitize account management	Provide customer self service
Close physical sales offices	1	9	5
Digitize account management	1/9	1	1/3
Provide customer self service	1/5	3	1

By processing this matrix mathematically, the AHP derives priorities for the concepts with respect to reducing operational costs. The priorities are measurements of their relative strengths, derived from the judgments of the decision makers as entered into the matrix.

In our example we're multiplying by a factor of 100 for our priorities.

	Close physical sales offices	Digitize account management	Provide customer self service	Priority
Close physical sales offices	1	9	5	72.66
Digitize account management	1/9	1	1/3	7.00
Provide customer self service	1/5	3	1	20.34
Total				100

As we did before with criteria, we can now compare the alternatives. The alternatives are compared within the context of the criteria. This time, we have 4 alternatives, so the number of pairs of concepts we need to rank increases.

For example, within the context of 'Providing customer self-service' which alternatives are best suited?

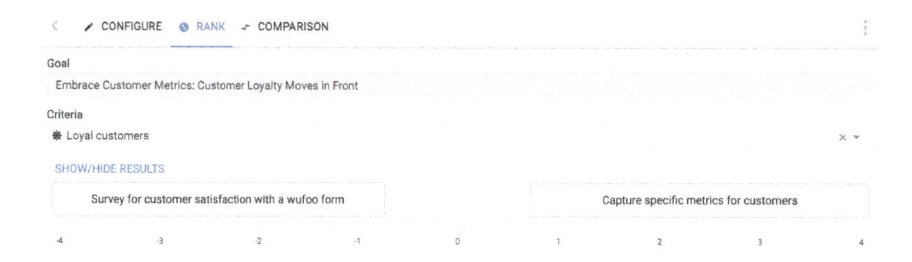

Figure 61: Example pairwise in Corso's platform

Figure 61 shows an example of how pairwise comparisons are presented in a tool that supports AHP.

The results of the pairwise are shown as follows:

Build web portal	7	Mobile platform for customer facing apps	1	Building a web portal is considerably more important than a mobile platform
Digitize paper based accounts	5	New account application	1	We need to digitize existing accounts for existing customers
Digitize paper based accounts	1	Build web portal	3	We can have a new web portal for new customers and then digitize existing customers later
Build web portal	3	New account application	1	The web portal is slightly more important than the new account application
New account application	7	Mobile platform for customer facing apps	1	We don't have to be mobile enabled right away to provide self service
Mobile platform for customer facing apps	1	Digitize paper based accounts	5	Digitizing our paper based accounts is majorly important compared to the mobile app

Again, we represent the alternatives in an AHP matrix:

	Build web portal	Mobile platform for customer facing apps	Digitize paper based accounts	New account application	Priority
Build web portal	1	7	3	3	39.60
Mobile platform for customer facing apps	1/7	1	1/5	1/7	4.20
Digitize paper based accounts	1/3	5	1	5	32.06
New account application	1/3	7	1/5	1	24.14
Total					100

As they did with the previous concepts, the community assigned to do the evaluation compares the pairs with respect to "Close physical sales offices" and "Digitize account management".

EXAMPLE COMPARISONS

Close physical sales offices

	Build web portal	Mobile platform for customer facing apps	Digitize paper based accounts	New account application	Priority
Build web portal	1	3	5	1/5	26.01
Mobile platform for customer facing apps	1/3	1	1/5	1/7	4.65
Digitize paper based accounts	1/5	5	1	1/3	18.47
New account application	5	9	3	1	50.88
Total					100

Digitize account management

	Build web portal	Mobile platform for customer facing apps	Digitize paper based accounts	New account application	Priority
Build web portal	1	3	1	5	29.44
Mobile platform for customer facing apps	1/3	1	1/5	1/7	4.94
Digitize paper based accounts	1/3	5	1	7	41.22
New account application	1/7	7	1/7	1	24.40
Total					100

It is worth remembering at this point, that we are only comparing the relative concepts with each other within the context of these criteria.

SYNTHESIZING FINAL PRIORITIES

Now that we know the priorities of the criteria with respect to the goal and the alternatives with respect to the criteria, we can now calculate the alternatives within the context of the goal.

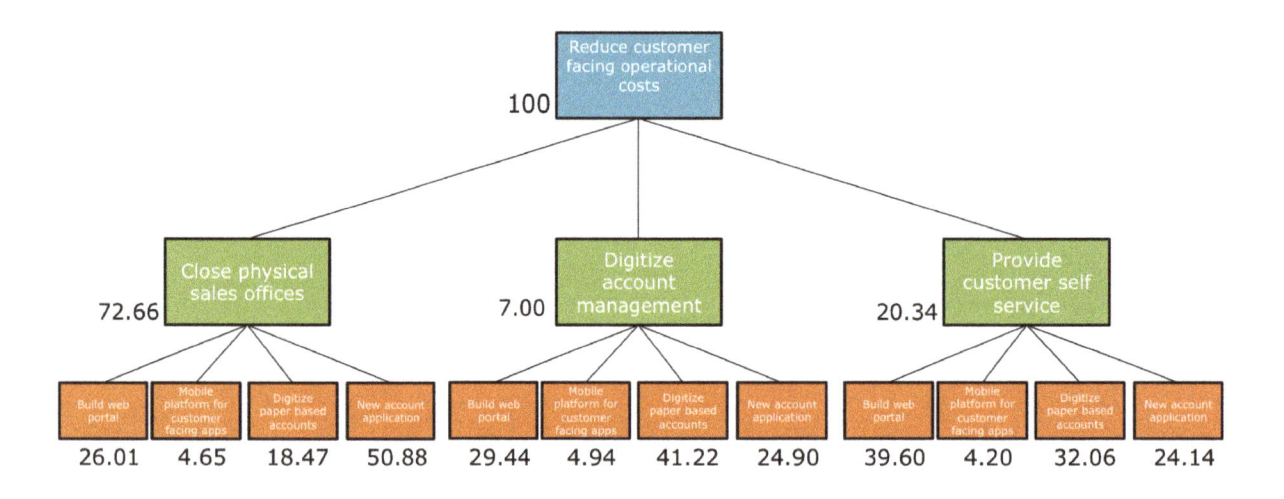

Figure 62: Synthesized priorities

In this example, we can now examine each alternative with respect to achieving the goal and calculate its priority based on:

1. The priority with respect to 'Close physical sales offices', multiplied by 'Close physical sales offices' with respect to the goal, and

2. The priority with respect to 'Digitize account management', multiplied by 'Digitize account management' with respect to the goal, and

3. The priority with respect to 'Provide customer self-service', multiplied by 'Provide customer self-service' with respect to the goal.

The priority column shows the product of priority of the criteria and priority of the alternative within the context of the criteria, we've then divided this by 100.

If we examine only 'Build web portal', we can see that the priority with respect to the goal is 28.96 which is calculated as follows:

'Build web portal' in the context of 'Provide customer self service' = 8.06, plus

'Build web portal' in the context of 'Close physical sales offices' = 18.89, plus

'Build web portal' in the context of 'Digitize account management' = 2.01,

which is a total of 28.96

Criteria	Priority v Goal	Alternative		Priority
Provide customer self service	20.34	Build web portal	39.60	8.06
		Mobile platform for customer facing apps	4.20	0.85
		Digitize paper based accounts	32.06	6.52
		New account application	24.14	4.91
			100.00	20.34
Close physical sales offices	72.66	Build web portal	26.01	18.89
		Mobile platform for customer facing apps	4.65	3.38
		Digitize paper based accounts	18.47	13.42
		New account application	50.88	36.97
			100.00	72.66
Digitize account management	7.00	Build web portal	28.72	2.01
		Mobile platform for customer facing apps	4.81	0.34
		Digitize paper based accounts	40.21	2.81
		New account application	26.26	1.84
	100.00		100.00	7.00
				100.00

The following pivot table is for the overall priorities for all of the concepts:

Sum of Overall Priority	Criteria			Grand Total
Alternatives	Close physical sales offices	Digitize account management	Provide customer self service	
Build web portal	18.89	2.01	8.06	28.96
Digitize paper based accounts	13.42	2.81	6.52	22.75
Mobile platform for customer facing apps	3.38	0.34	0.85	4.57
New account application	36.97	1.84	4.91	43.72
Grand Total	72.66	7.00	20.34	100.00

DECISION MAKING WITH AHP

Based on the communities' choice of decision criteria, their judgement on the relative importance of each and on their judgements about each concept with respect to each criterion, the New account application work package is by far the most suitable project to carry out.

Because the community has used AHP, it's easy to trace the decision-making steps and justify the outcome.

The AHP process can be revisited when necessary and changes made if appropriate to suit the end goal.

In larger communities where some members have more importance than others, you may find it useful to add a weighting factor for the relative importance of the member that is voting, thereby ranking according to preference and importance of voter.

APPENDIX B

ARCHIMATE 2.1 REFERENCE GUIDE

CORE VIEWPOINTS

ORGANIZATION VIEWPOINT

The organization viewpoint focuses on the (internal) organization of a company. It can be represented hierarchically or as a box in box view.

The organization viewpoint is used to identify competencies, authority, and responsibilities in an organization.

The meta-types for the organization viewpoint are:

> Actor, Business collaboration, Business interface, Location, Role

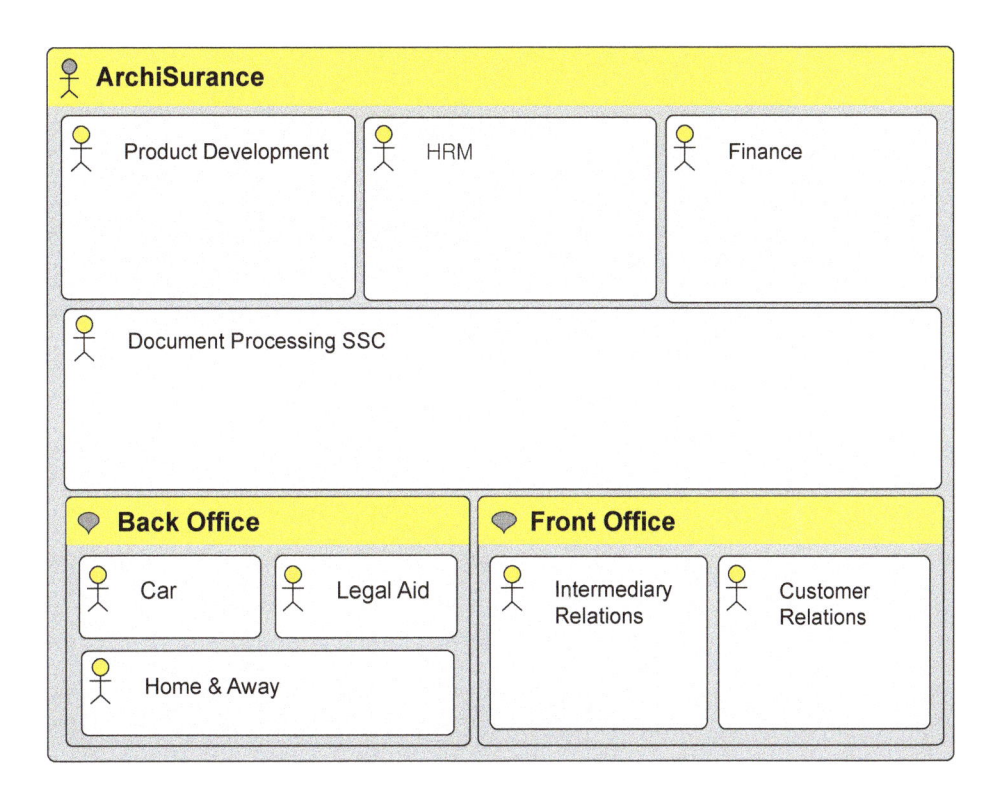

ACTOR CO-OPERATION VIEWPOINT

The Actor Co-operation viewpoint focuses on the relationships of actors with each other and their environment.

This viewpoint is also used to show how a number of cooperating actors or application components may work together to realize a business process.

The meta-types for this viewpoint are:

Actor, Business collaboration, Business interface, Business service, Application service, Application interface, Application component, Role

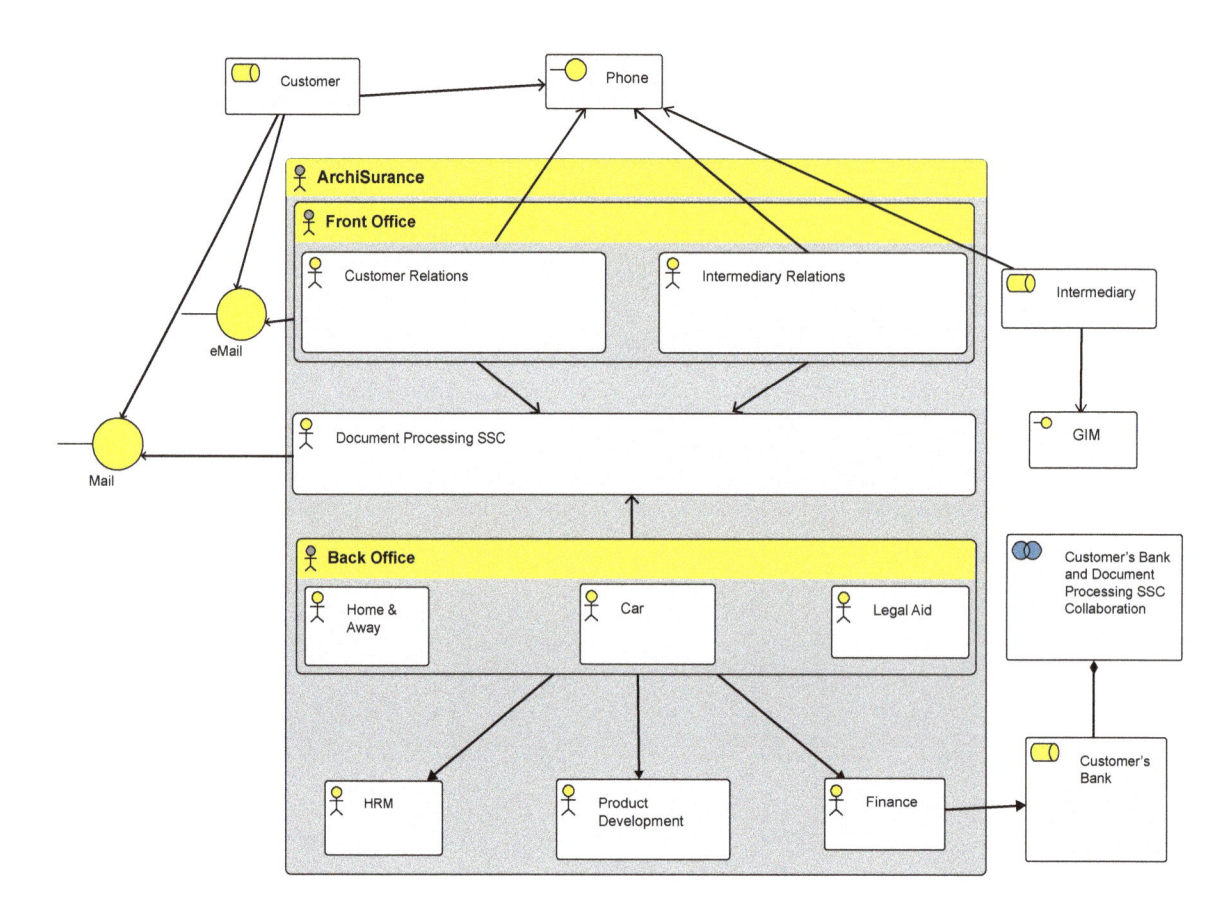

BUSINESS FUNCTION VIEWPOINT

The Business Function viewpoint shows the main business functions of an organization and their relationships in terms of the flows of information, value, or goods between them.

Business functions represent the most stable operations of an organization.

This view provides a high level insight into the operations of a company.

The meta-types for this viewpoint are:

Business Function, Role and Actor

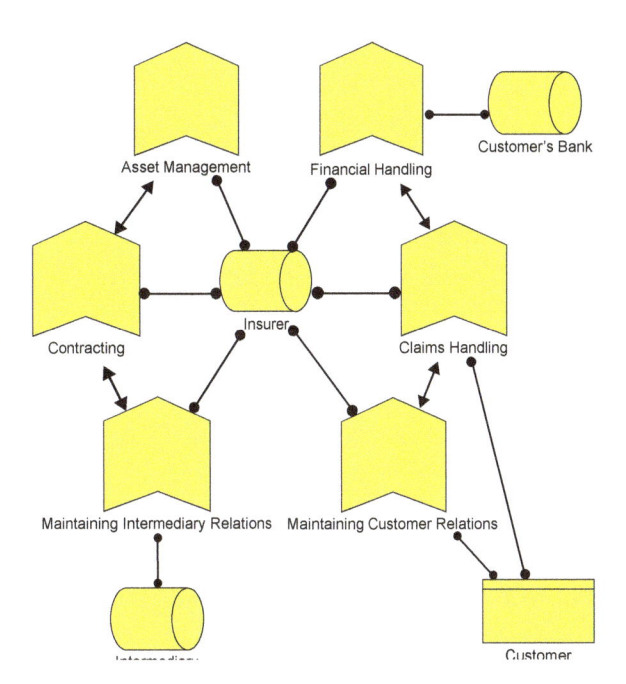

BUSINESS PROCESS CO-OPERATION VIEWPOINT

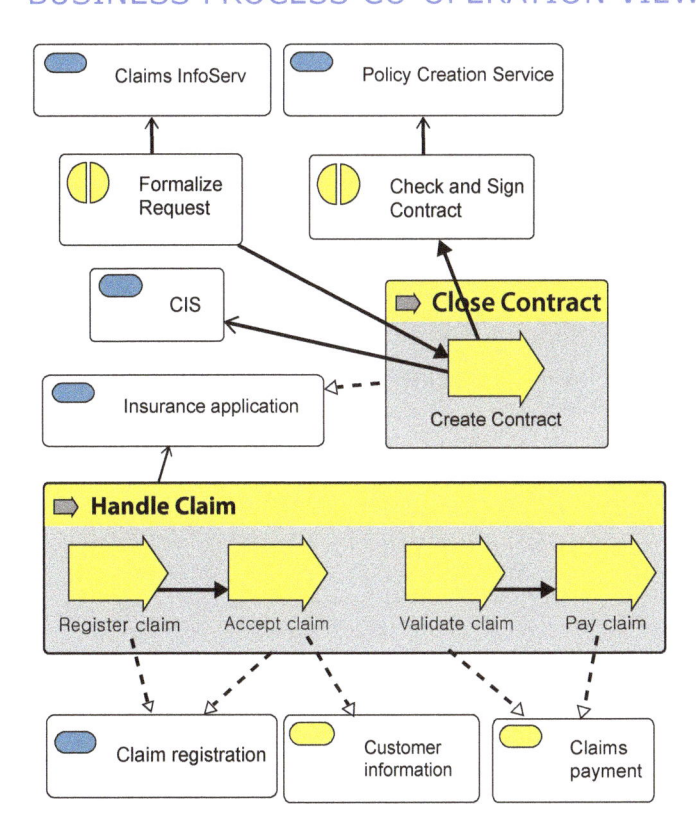

The business process co-operation viewpoint is used to show the relationships between one or more business processes with each other and/or with their environment.

The meta-types for this viewpoint are:

Business service, Representation, Business object, Business process, Business function, Role, Actor, Business event, Business interaction, Business collaboration, Location and Application service.

BUSINESS PROCESS VIEWPOINT

The Business Process viewpoint is used to show the high-level structure and composition of one or more business processes.

ArchiMate® provides many of the same underlying concepts as the business process modeling notation (BPMN). ArchiMate® can be used very easily in conjunction with BPMN as an alternative viewpoint.

The meta-types for this viewpoint are:

Business service, Representation, Business object, Business process, Business function, Role, Actor, Business event, Business interaction, Business collaboration, Location and Application service.

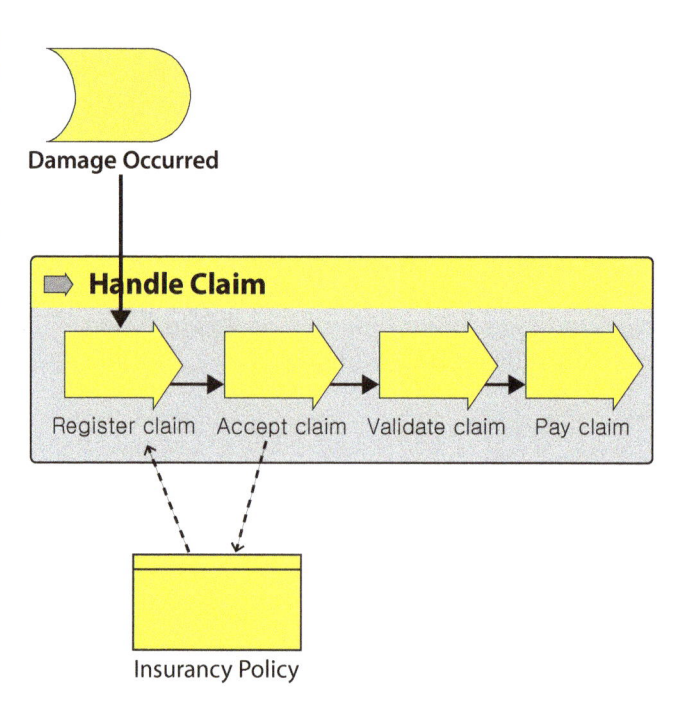

PRODUCT VIEWPOINT

The Product viewpoint depicts the value that these products offer to the customers or other external parties involved and shows the composition of one or more products in terms of the constituting (business or application) services.

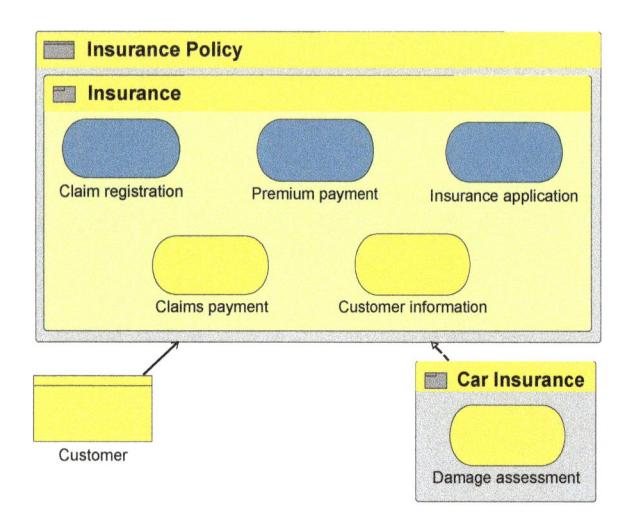

A product viewpoint is typically used in product development to design a product by designing services that a customer expects from it.

The meta-types for this viewpoint are:

Product, Value, Contract, Business service, Business interface, Business event, Business process, Business function, Business interaction, Role, Actor, Application service, Application interface and Application component.

APPLICATION BEHAVIOR VIEWPOINT

The Application Behavior viewpoint describes the internal behavior of an application; e.g., as it realizes one or more application services.

This viewpoint is useful in the designing how applications behave and how applications functionally overlap.

The meta-types for this viewpoint are:

> Application service, Application interface, Data object, Application function, Application component, Application collaboration and Application interaction.

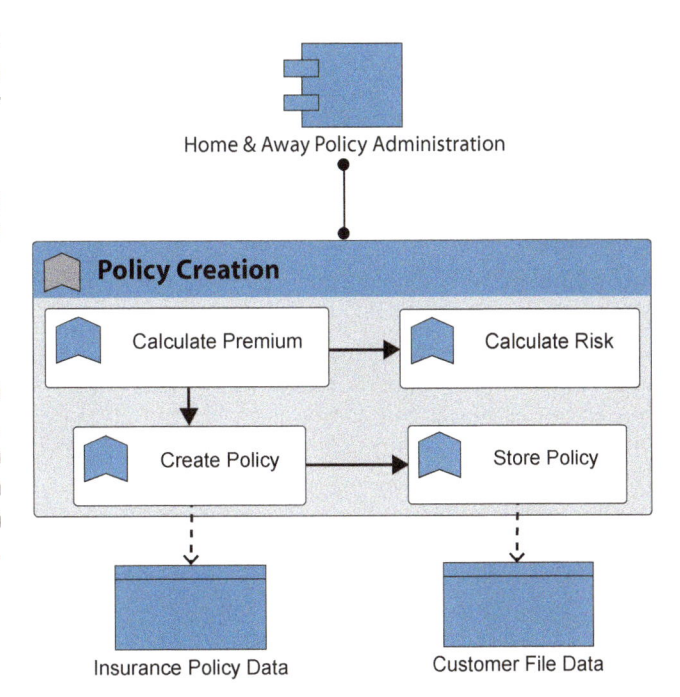

APPLICATION CO-OPERATION VIEWPOINT

The Application Co-operation viewpoint describes the relationships between applications components in terms of the information flows between them, or in terms of the services they offer and use.

This viewpoint is often used to create an **application landscape** view of the organization.

The meta-types for this viewpoint are:

> Application service, Application interface, Data object, Application function, Application component, Application collaboration, Application interaction and Location.

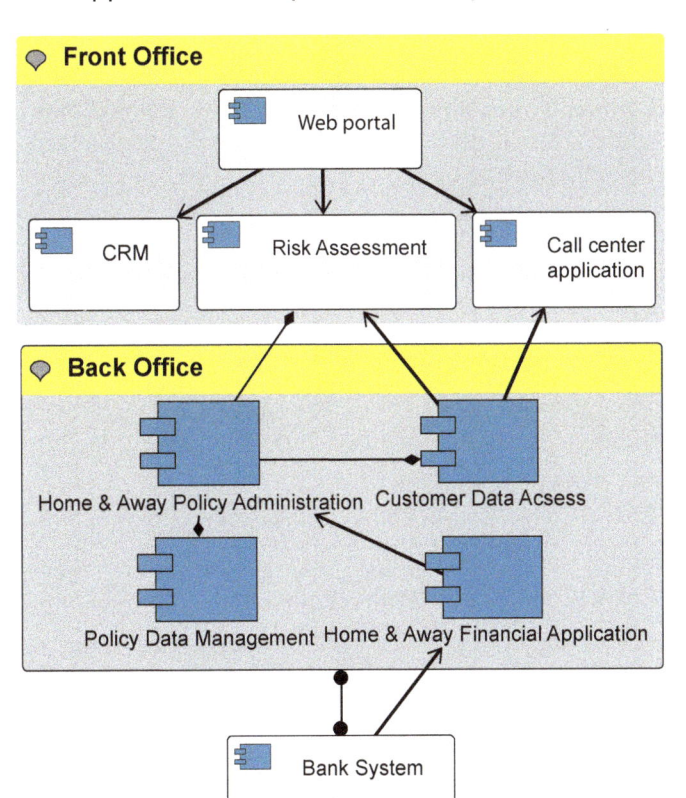

Page | **143**

APPLICATION STRUCTURE VIEWPOINT

The Application Structure viewpoint shows the structure of one or more applications or components.

The main use of this viewpoint is to understand the main architecture of applications and their associated data.

The meta-types for this viewpoint are:

Application interface, Data object, Application component and Application collaboration.

APPLICATION USAGE VIEWPOINT

The Application Usage viewpoint describes how applications are used to support one or more business processes, and how they are used by other applications.

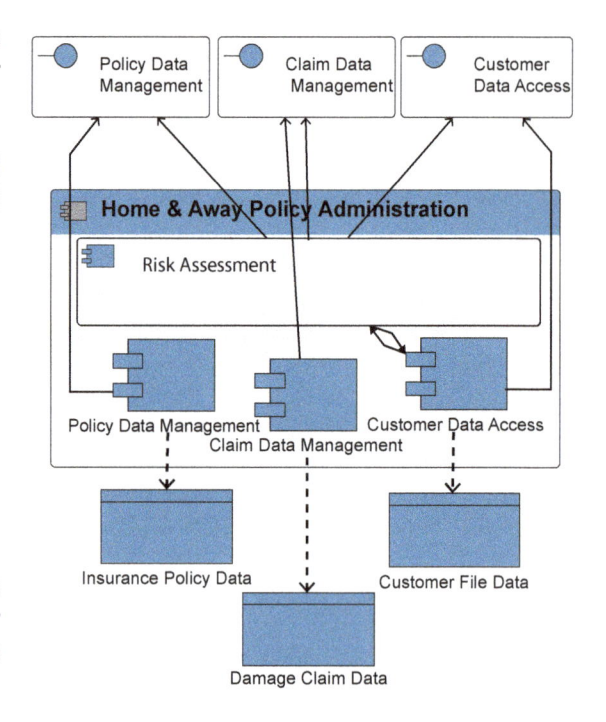

This viewpoint is useful when designing an application through identification of the required business services and processes, or in designing processes by describing the application services available to it.

The meta-types for this viewpoint are:

Business event, Business object, Business process, Business interaction, Business function, Role, Application service, Data object, Application interface, Application component and Application collaboration.

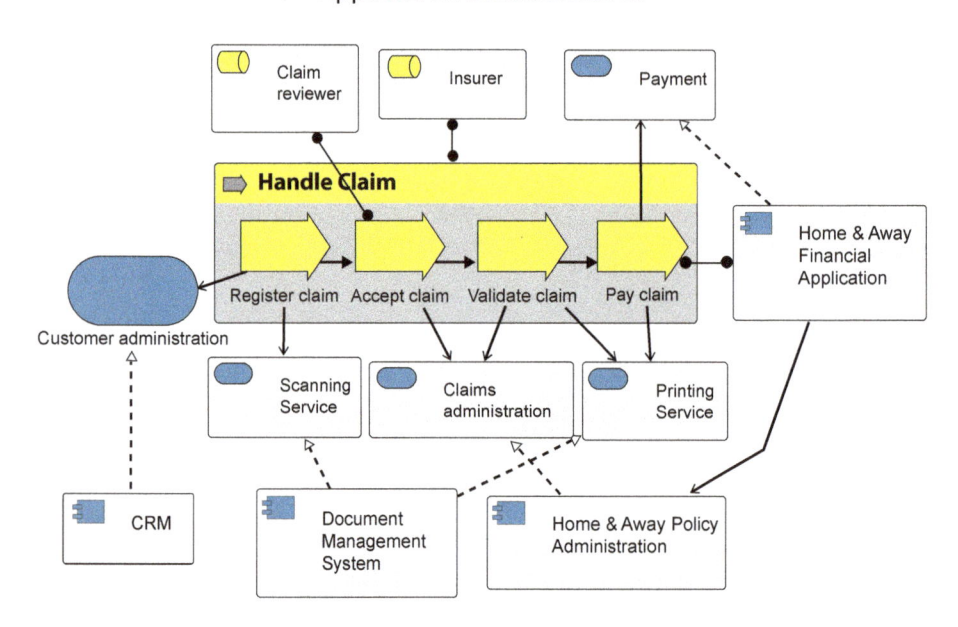

INFRASTRUCTURE VIEWPOINT

The Infrastructure viewpoint contains the software and hardware infrastructure elements supporting the application layer, such as physical devices, networks, or system software (e.g., operating systems, databases, and middleware).

This viewpoint is ideal to describe the infrastructure and its associations to locations.

The meta-types for this viewpoint are:

Artifact, Infrastructure service, Infrastructure interface, Infrastructure function, Node, Communication path, Location, System software, Device and Network.

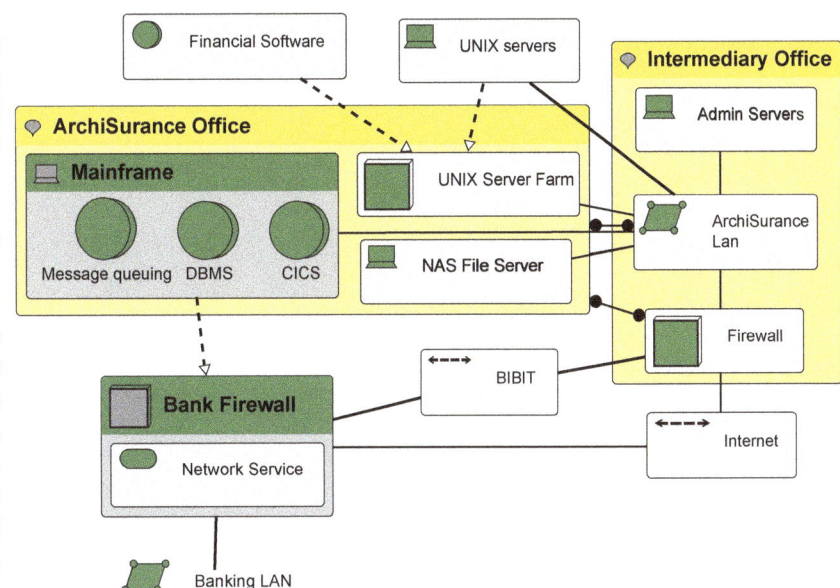

INFRASTRUCTURE USAGE VIEWPOINT

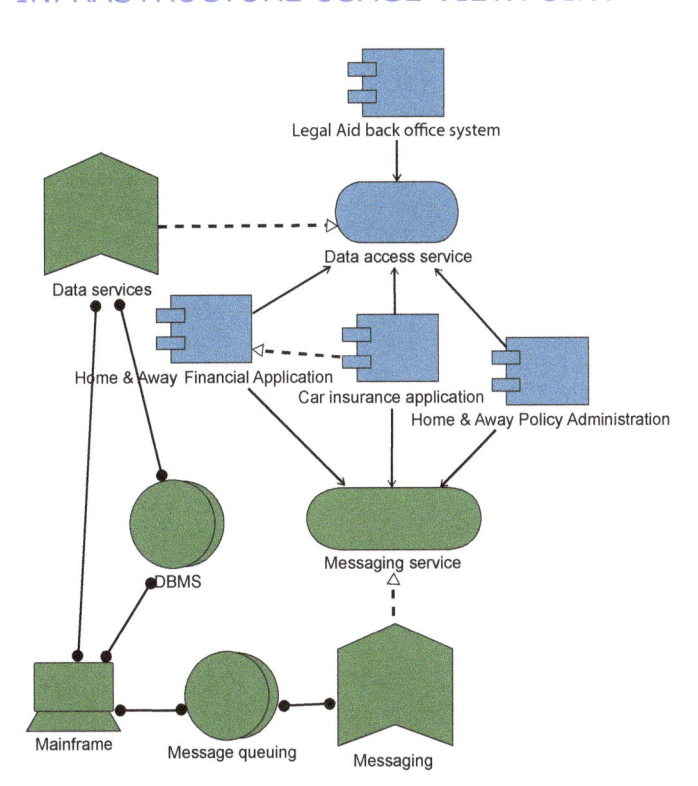

The Infrastructure Usage viewpoint shows how applications are supported by the software and hardware infrastructure: the devices deliver the infrastructure services; system software and networks are provided to the applications.

This viewpoint is important in analyzing quality, performance and scalability as it relates the physical infrastructure to the applications.

The meta-types for this viewpoint are:

Application function, Application component, Infrastructure service, Infrastructure interface, Infrastructure function, Node, Communication path, System software, Device and Network

IMPLEMENTATION AND DEPLOYMENT VIEWPOINT

The Implementation and Deployment viewpoint shows how one or more applications are realized on the infrastructure.

This viewpoint is important when examining dependencies between physical infrastructure and applications.

The meta-types for this viewpoint are:

Application collaboration, Data object, Application component, Artifact, Infrastructure service, Node, Communication path, System software, Device and Network.

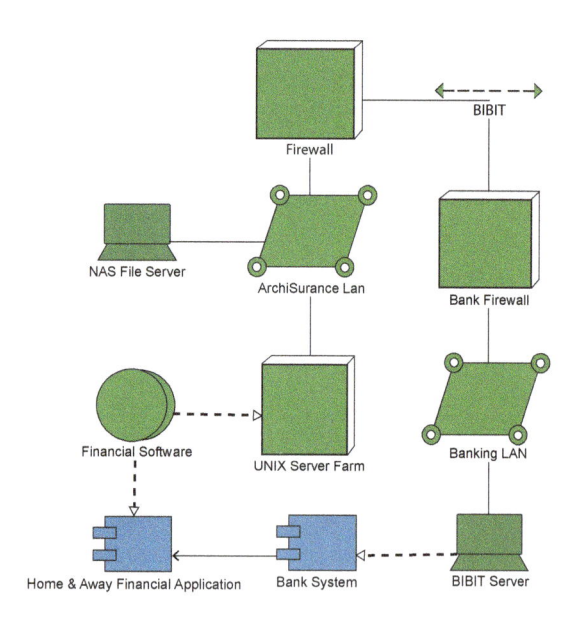

INFORMATION STRUCTURE VIEWPOINT

The Information Structure viewpoint is comparable to the traditional information models created in the development of almost any information system.

This viewpoint shows the structure of information and their relationships. It also maps business level data, to application level data and how these map to the underlying infrastructure.

The meta-types for this viewpoint are:

Meaning, Representation, Business object, Data object and Artifact.

SERVICE REALIZATION VIEWPOINT

The Service Realization viewpoint is used to show how one or more business services are realized by the underlying processes (and sometimes by application components).

This viewpoint provides a bridge between the product and business process view.

The meta-types for this viewpoint are:

Business service, Business event, Business collaboration, Business object, Business process, Business function, Business interaction, Role, Actor, Data object, Application service, Application component and Application collaboration

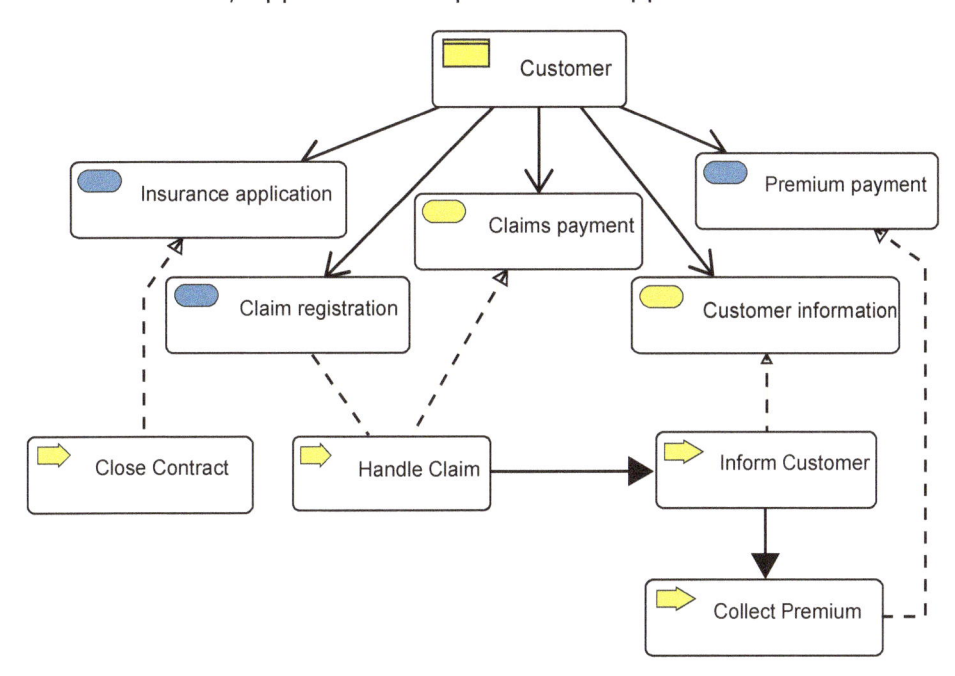

LAYERED VIEWPOINT

The layered viewpoint pictures several layers and aspects of enterprise architecture in one diagram.

This view is used to support analysis and impact of change on the model.

The meta-types for this viewpoint are all core concepts and associations.

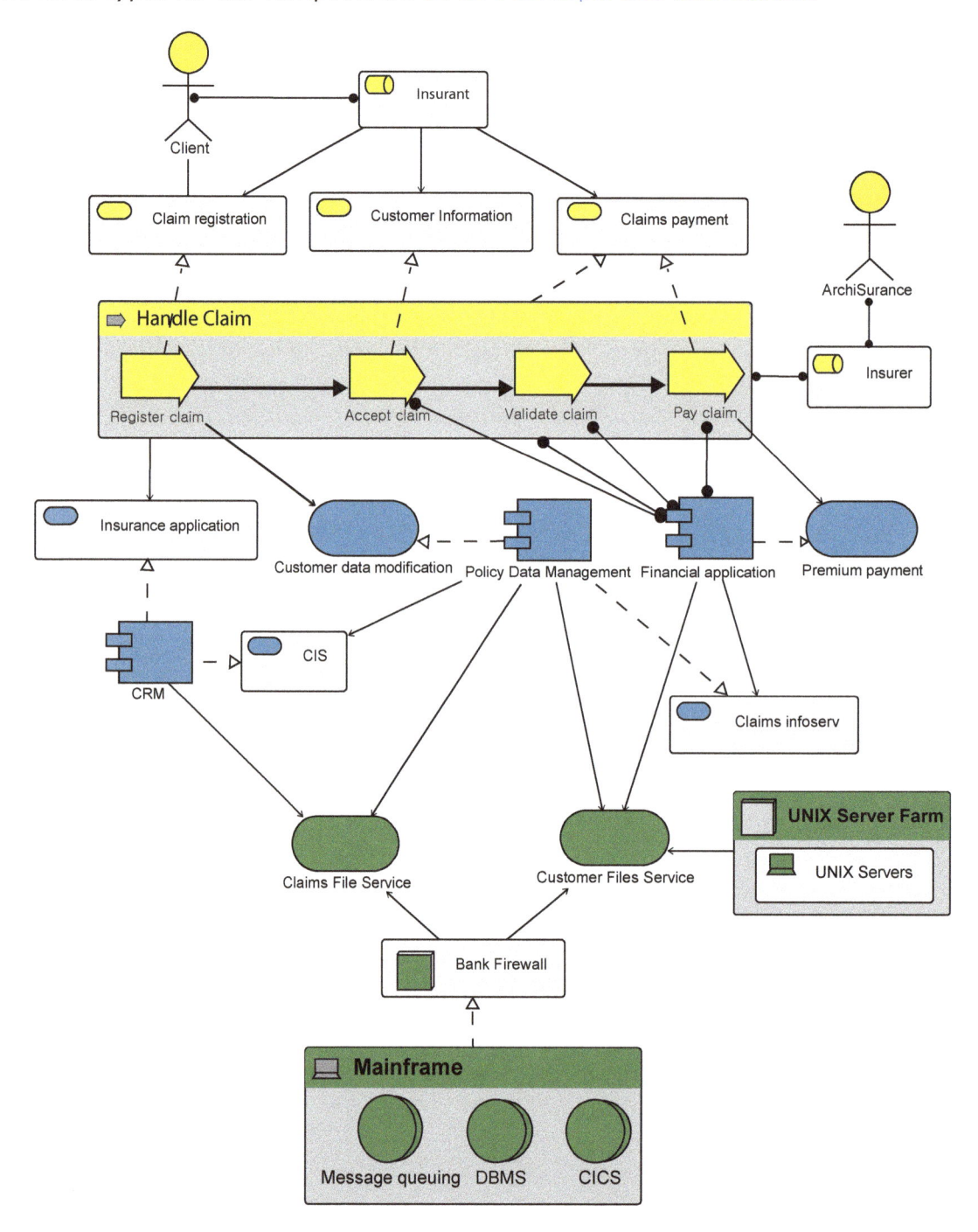

MOTIVATION EXTENSION VIEWPOINTS

STAKEHOLDER VIEWPOINT

The stakeholder viewpoint allows the analyst to model the stakeholders and the internal and external drivers for change.

The stakeholder viewpoint focuses on the stakeholders that are actually special types of role, drivers, the assessments of the drivers and initial goals that address the drivers and assessments.

The meta-types for this viewpoint are:

> Stakeholder (Role), Driver, Goal, Assessment

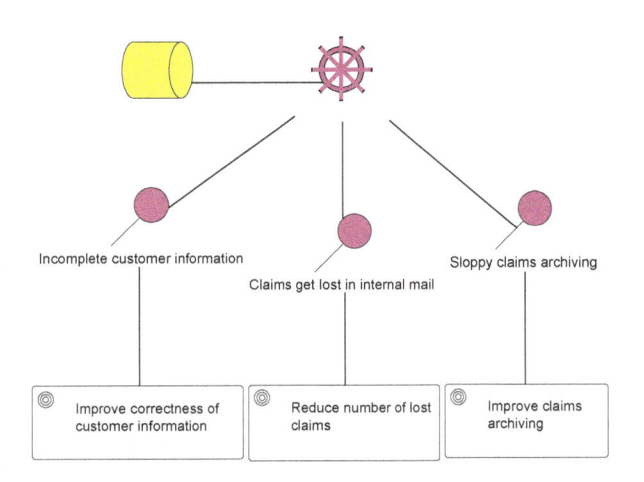

GOAL REALIZATION VIEWPOINT

Focuses on refining the initial, high-level goals into more concrete (sub-) goals using the aggregation relationship, and finally into requirements and constraints using the realization relationship.

Principles can be shown that aid the refinement of goals into requirements.

The refinement of goals is expressed through aggregation and composition associations. Thereby goals can be composed of other goals.

The meta-types for this viewpoint are:

> Goal, Requirement, Principle and Constraint.

GOAL CONTRIBUTION VIEWPOINT

Focuses on modeling and analyzing the influence relationships between goals and requirements.

This viewpoint is typically used after goals and sub goals have been defined and are used to show the impact that goals have on one another so that conflicts can be resolved.

The meta-types for this viewpoint are:

Goal, Requirement, Principle and Constraint.

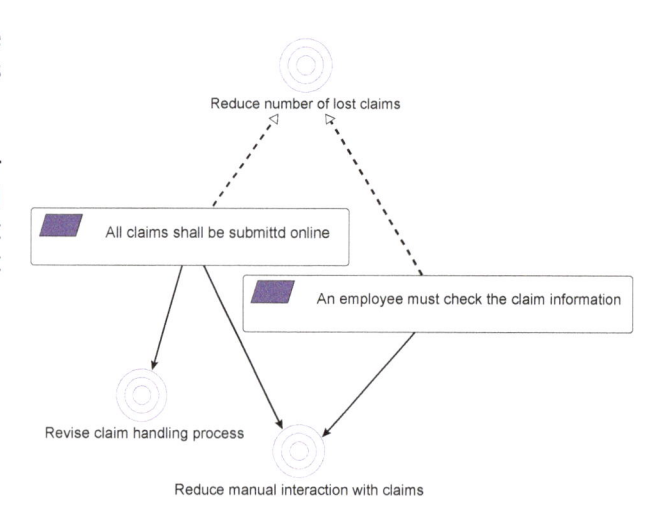

PRINCIPLES VIEWPOINT

Focuses on modeling the relevant principles and the goals that motivate those principles.

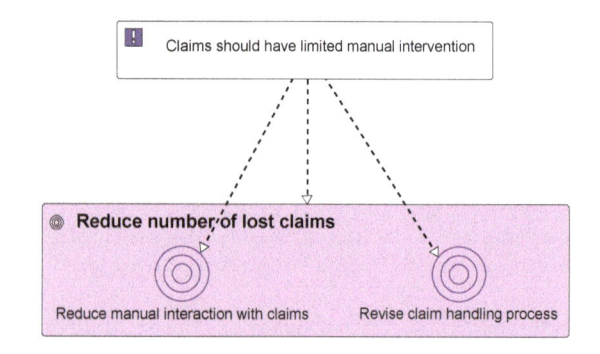

Principles can influence each other positively and negatively.

Positive and negative (+,-) can be marked on the associations.

The meta-types for this viewpoint are:

Goal, Principle

REQUIREMENTS REALIZATION VIEWPOINT

Focuses on modeling the realization of requirements and constraints by means of core elements, such as actors, services, processes, application components, etc.

This viewpoint is typically used to model requirements and how they are realized and to refine requirements into more detailed requirements.

The meta-types for this viewpoint are:

Goal, Requirement, Constraint and any Core element.

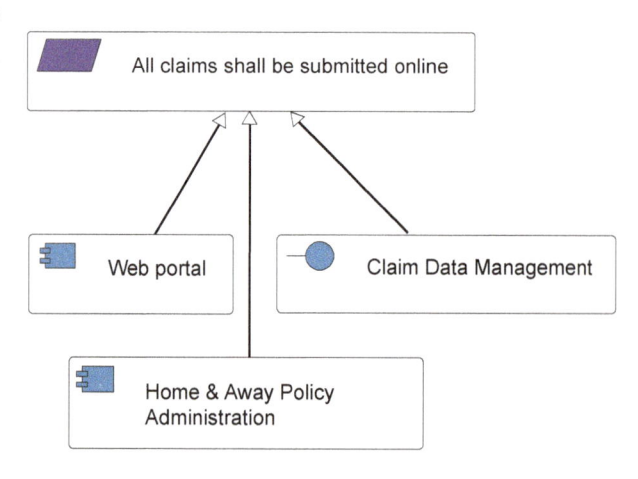

MOTIVATION VIEWPOINT

Covers the entire motivational aspect and allows one to use all motivational elements.

Typically the motivation viewpoint is used to model the complete or partial view of motivation including stakeholders (roles).

This view is similar to the business motivation model used in other frameworks.

The meta-types for this viewpoint are:

Stakeholder (role), Driver, Assessment, Goal, Principle, Requirement and Constraint.

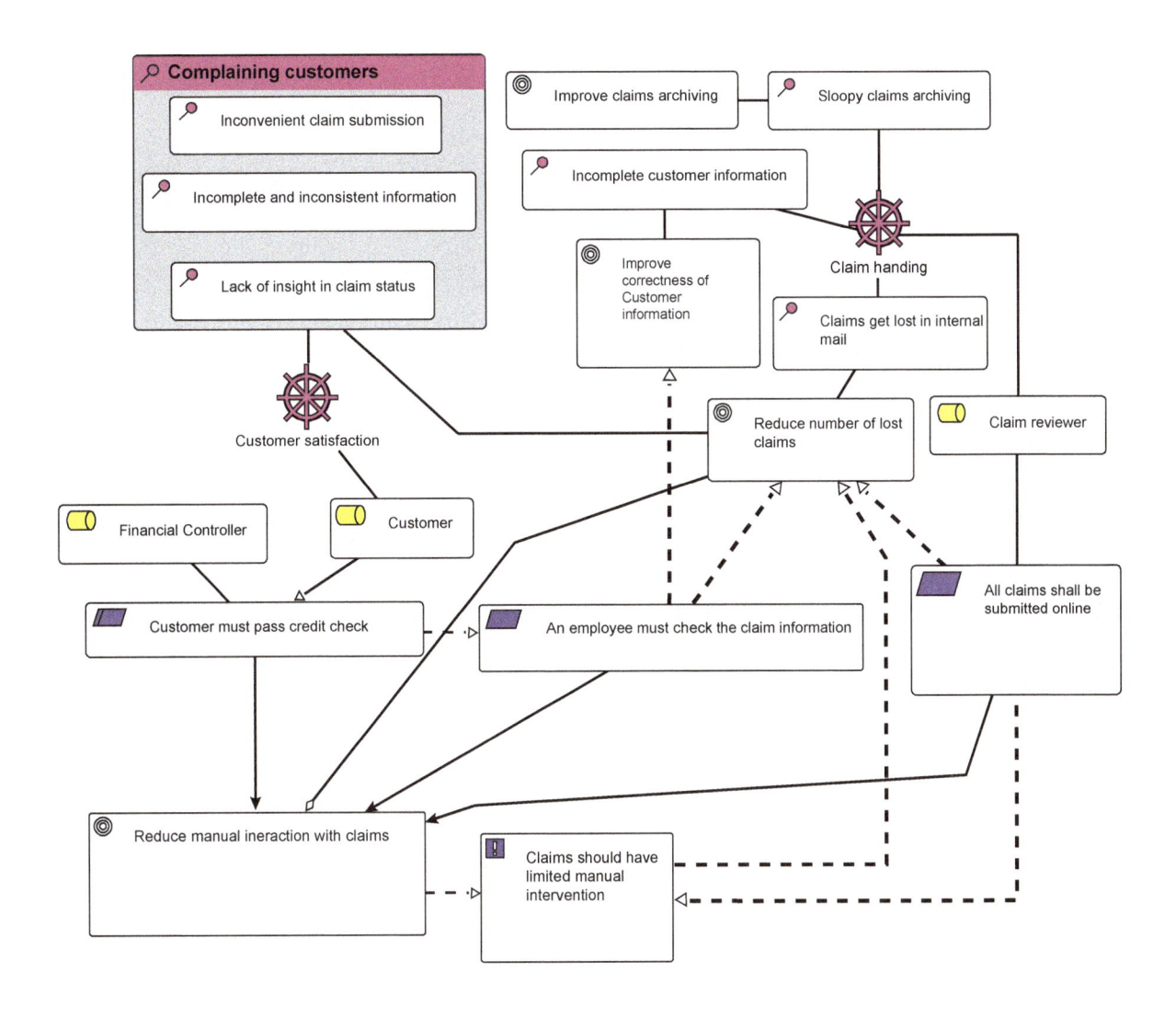

IMPLEMENTATION AND MIGRATION EXTENSION VIEWPOINTS

PROJECT VIEWPOINT

Primarily used to model the management of architecture change.

This viewpoint is used to show the work packages and their deliverables. It also shows the goals that the work packages realize and the stakeholders (Roles) involved.

The meta-types for this viewpoint are:

Goal, Deliverable, Work package, Role and Actor.

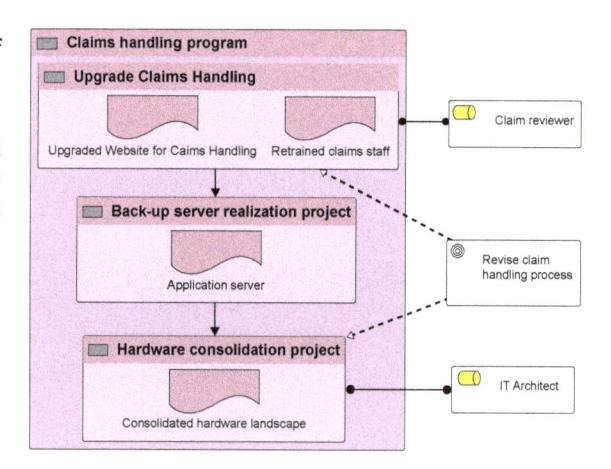

MIGRATION VIEWPOINT

Used to model the transition from an existing architecture to target architecture.

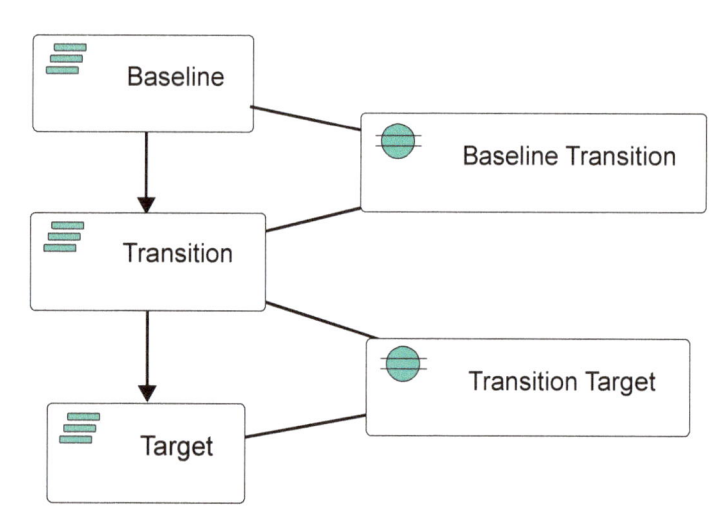

This viewpoint represents the migration planning from a current state to a future state architecture.

This viewpoint is ideal for modeling "as is" and "to be" states of the architecture.

The use of this viewpoint is described in more detail in the workspaces topic.

The meta-types for this viewpoint are:

Gap and Plateau.

IMPLEMENTATION AND MIGRATION VIEWPOINT

The implementation and migration viewpoint is used to relate programs and projects to the parts of the architecture that they implement.

This view provides the scope to work packages and the plateaus that they support. Any concepts or core elements affected by a work package or plateau can be shown here.

This viewpoint can be use in combination with the programs and projects viewpoint and the implementation and migration viewpoint to support portfolio management.

The meta-types for this viewpoint are:

Location, Role, Actor, Work package, Deliverable, Requirement, Constraint, Goal, Plateau, Gap and any Core element.

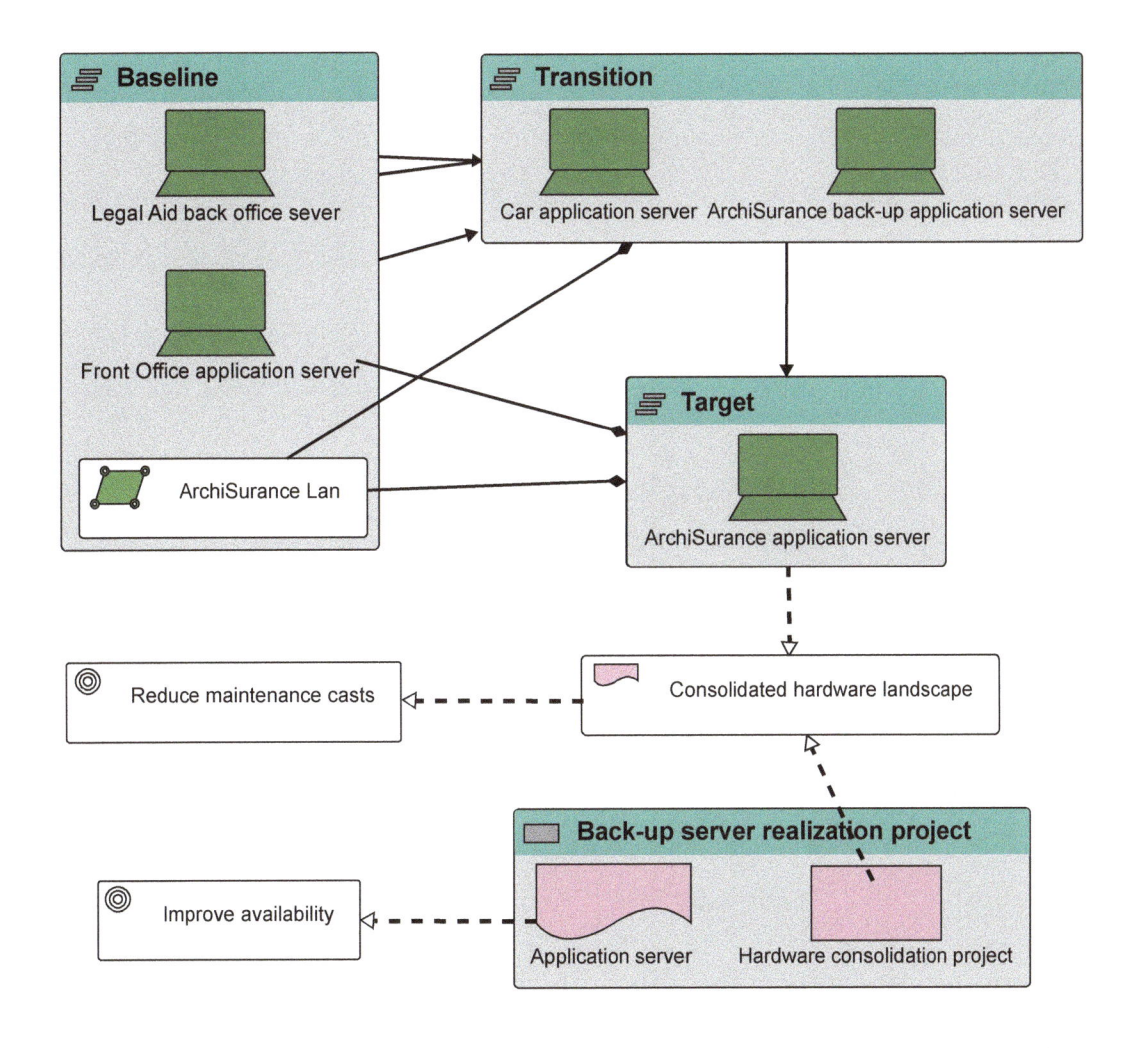

CAPABILITY BASED PLANNING VIEWPOINTS

BUSINESS CAPABILITY VIEWPOINT

The business capability viewpoint is used to describe one or more business capabilities, their hierarchy and their associations with each other including inputs or outputs.

The hierarchy is represented with an aggregation or composition association.

The viewpoint may also include drivers and metrics for each capability as well as the stakeholder (Role) that supports it.

The hierarchy is often represented as 'box in box' for simplicity for communication with other stakeholders. However, a hierachy can be used instead.

The meta-types for this viewpoint are:

Deliverable, Business capability, Stakeholder (Role), Driver and Metric.

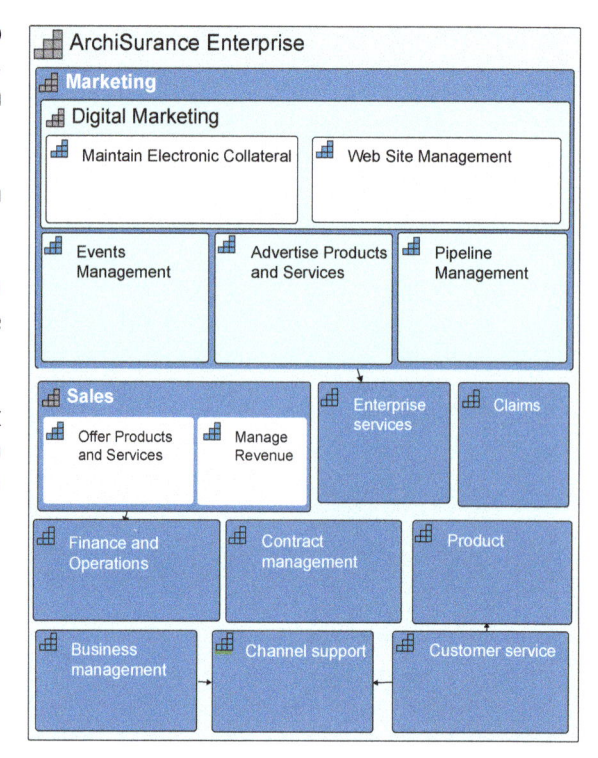

BUSINESS CAPABILITY INCREMENT VIEWPOINT

This viewpoint can show how a project can bring about one or more capability increments and a single increment can be realized by one or more projects.

This view is usually for a single capability increment and includes the motivation aspects of the increment.

The meta-types for this viewpoint are:

Driver, Assessment, Metric, Goal, Work package, Deliverable, Capability increment, Plateau and Business capability.

OTHER USEFUL VIEWPOINTS

As mentioned previously views are custom to each organization and their stakeholders. The views that are defined for the ArchiMate specification are example views only. In this section, we are showing a couple of views that are clients have found useful.

IDEA TO DELIVERY VIEWPOINT

The idea to delivery viewpoint is used to show how an idea is realized through to implementation.

The motivation behind the idea and work packages is included.

This view is ideal to those users modeling both Innovation Management and Agile EA concepts.

The meta-types for this viewpoint are:

Idea, Requirement, Goal, Driver, Assessment, Constraint, Principle, Deliverable, Work package and any Core element.

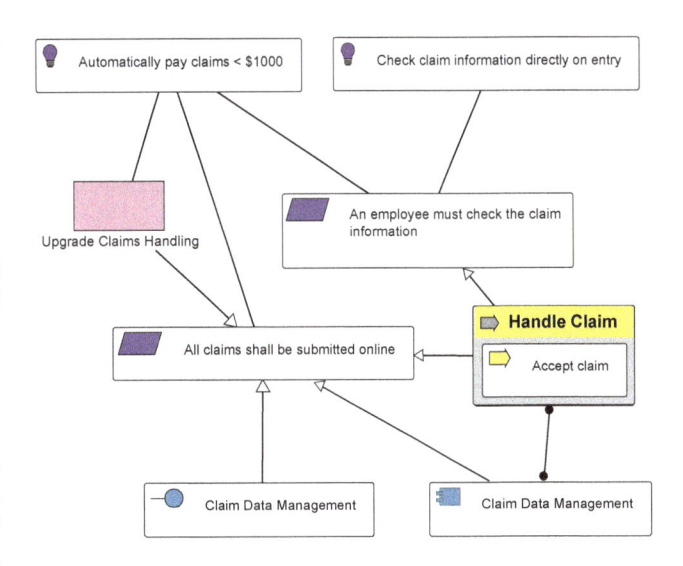

CAPABILITY TO APPLICATION COMPONENT VIEWPOINT

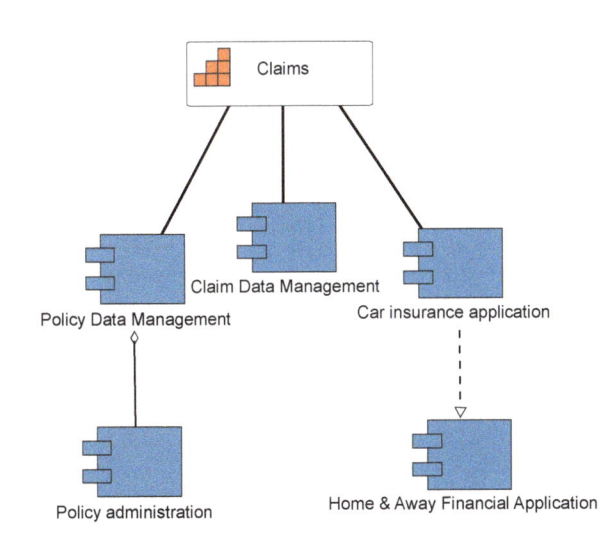

Provides a view of how business capabilities are associated with application components. This view is ideal for users that want to show application portfolios and how they are linked to the capabilities of the business.

The meta-types for this viewpoint are:

Application component and Business capability

For a complete guide on ArchiMate, please refer to the ArchiMate 2.1 specification available from the open group.

META-TYPE TO VIEWPOINT MATRIX

Meta-types \ Viewpoints	Actor Co-operation	Application Behavior	Application Co-operation	Application Structure	Application Usage	Business Capability Increment	Business Capability	Business Function	Business Process Co-operation	Business Process Viewpoint	Capability to Application Component	Goal Contribution	Goal Realization	Idea to Delivery	Implementation and Deployment	Implementation and Migration	Information Structure	Infrastructure	Infrastructure Usage	Layered	Migration	Motivation	Organization	Principles	Product	Project	Requirements Realization	Service Realization	Stakeholder
Actor	■							■	■	■				■		■				■			■		■		■	■	
Application collaboration		■	■	■	■									■		■				■							■	■	
Application component	■	■	■	■	■						■			■		■			■	■					■		■	■	
Application function		■	■	■										■		■				■									
Application interaction		■	■	■										■		■				■									
Application interface	■	■	■	■	■									■		■				■							■	■	
Application service	■	■	■		■									■		■				■							■	■	
Artifact														■	■	■	■	■		■									
Assessment						■								■								■							■
Business capability						■	■				■			■						■					■				
Business collaboration	■							■	■	■				■						■							■	■	
Business event					■				■	■				■						■									
Business function					■			■		■				■						■									
Business interaction					■			■	■	■				■						■									
Business interface	■				■					■				■						■			■				■	■	
Business object					■					■				■			■			■									
Business process					■				■	■				■						■									
Business service	■				■				■	■				■						■					■		■	■	
Capability increment						■								■															
Communication path														■	■	■		■	■	■									
Constraint												■	■	■								■					■		
Contract																									■				
Data object	■	■	■	■										■		■	■			■							■	■	
Deliverable					■	■								■		■										■			
Device														■	■	■		■	■	■									
Driver					■	■								■						■		■							■
Gap																■					■								
Goal					■							■	■	■						■		■					■		■
Idea																													
Infrastructure function														■	■	■		■	■	■							■		
Infrastructure interface														■	■	■		■	■	■							■		
Infrastructure service														■	■	■		■	■	■									
Location					■				■	■				■						■			■						
Meaning																	■												
Metric						■	■																						
Network														■	■	■		■	■	■									
Node														■	■	■		■	■	■							■		
Plateau						■										■					■								
Principle												■	■	■								■		■					
Product																									■				
Representation									■	■				■			■			■									
Requirement													■	■								■					■		
Role	■				■			■	■	■				■						■			■				■	■	■
System software														■	■	■		■	■	■									
Value																									■				
Work package						■								■		■				■						■			

ARCHIMATE CONCEPTS

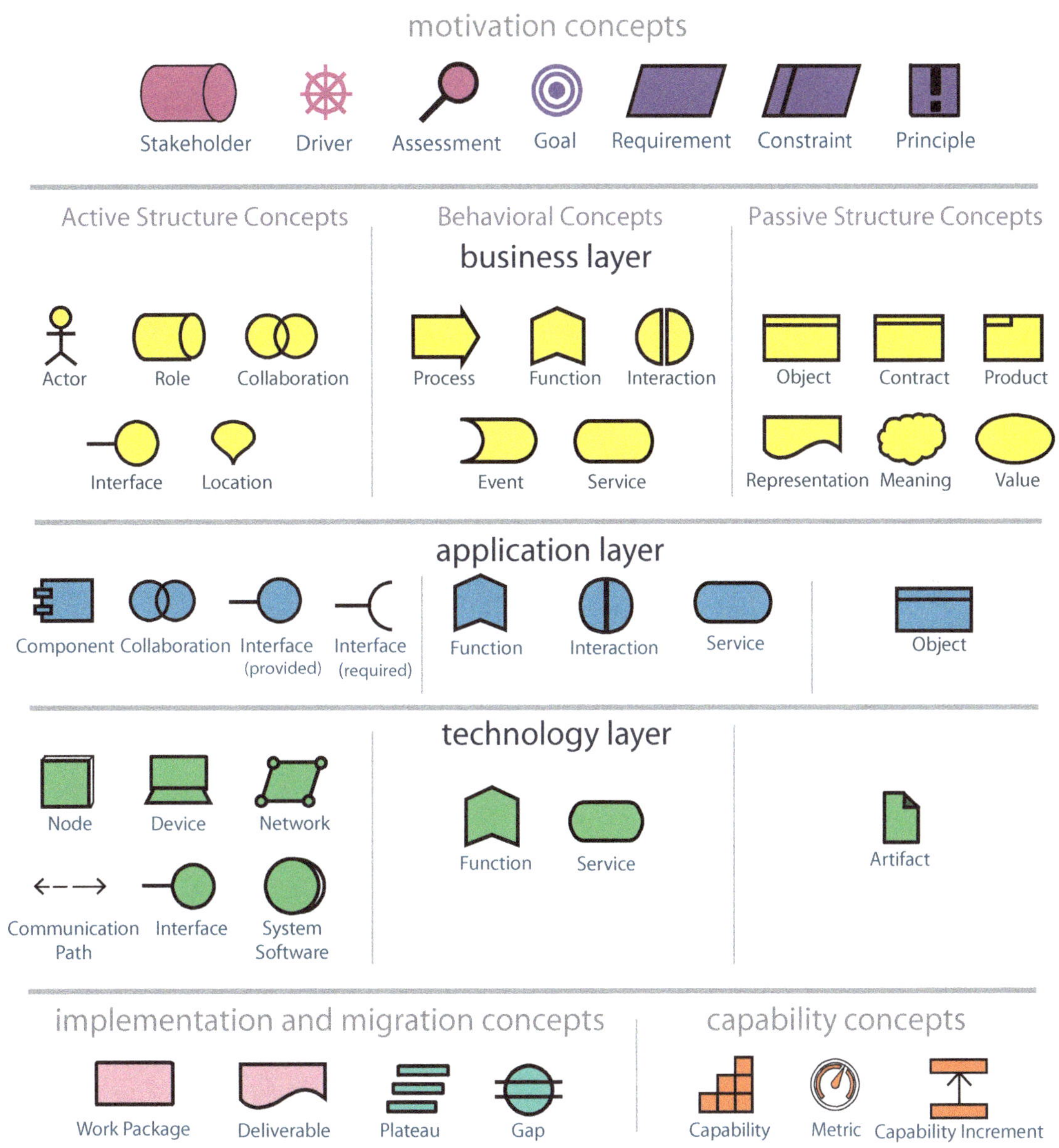

motivation concepts

Stakeholder, Driver, Assessment, Goal, Requirement, Constraint, Principle

Active Structure Concepts | Behavioral Concepts | Passive Structure Concepts

business layer

Actor, Role, Collaboration, Interface, Location

Process, Function, Interaction, Event, Service

Object, Contract, Product, Representation, Meaning, Value

application layer

Component, Collaboration, Interface (provided), Interface (required), Function, Interaction, Service, Object

technology layer

Node, Device, Network, Communication Path, Interface, System Software, Function, Service, Artifact

implementation and migration concepts

Work Package, Deliverable, Plateau, Gap

capability concepts

Capability, Metric, Capability Increment

associations

Relationship Name	From Relationship	Line Graphic	To Relationship
Specialization	is specialization of	——▷	has specialization of
Aggregation	is aggregation of	◇——	is part of an aggregation of
Composition	comprises	◆——	is part of
Assignment	assigned to	●——	assigned from
Realization	realizes	---▷	realized by

Relationship Name	From Relationship	Line Graphic	To Relationship
Triggering	triggers	——▶	triggered by
Flow	flows to	---▶	flows from
Use	used by	——▷	uses
Access	accesses	——▶	accessed by
Association	associated to	——	associated from

Page | 157

CORE META-MODEL

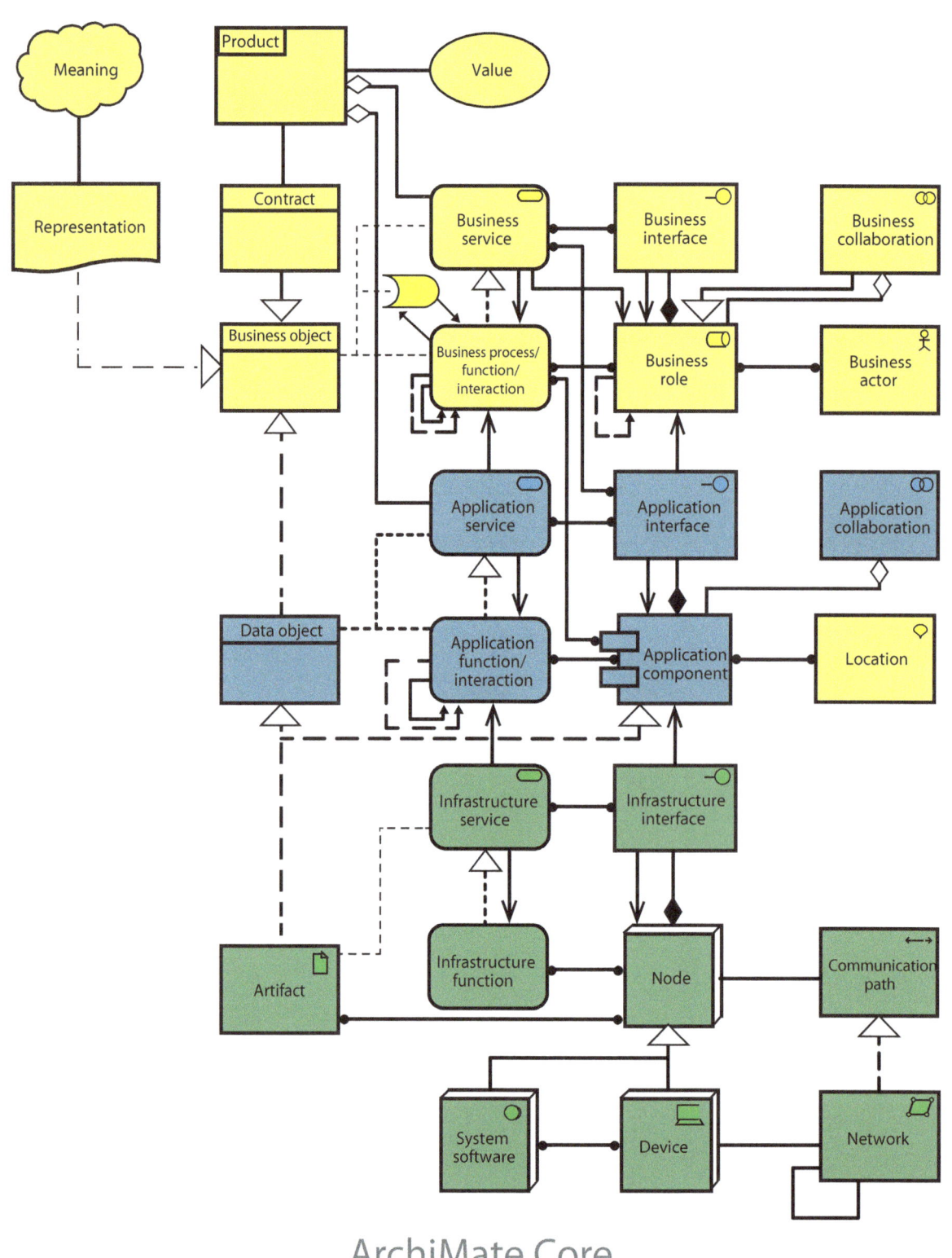

ArchiMate Core Metamodel*

* does not include all associations

META-MODEL EXTENSIONS

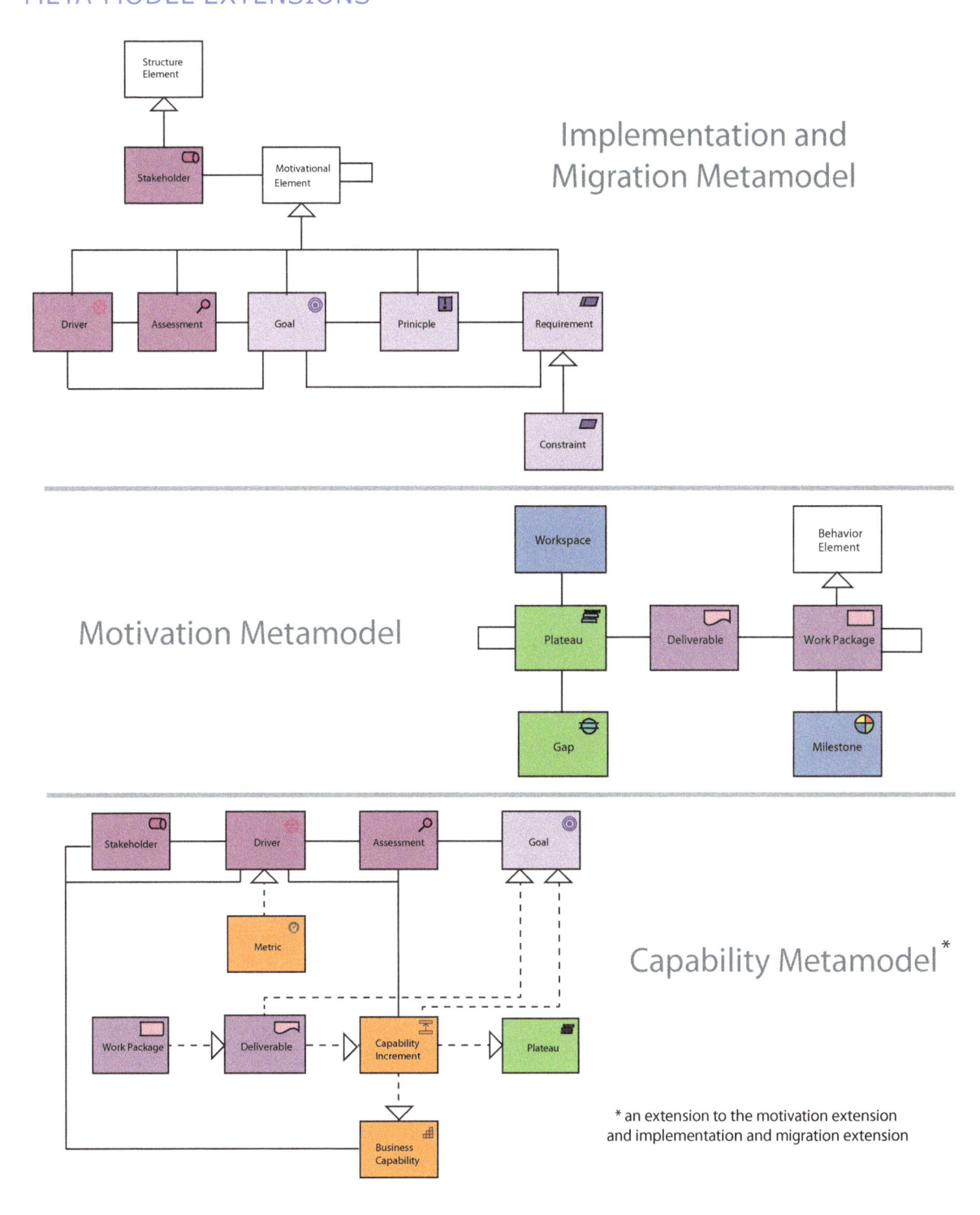

Implementation and Migration Metamodel

Motivation Metamodel

Capability Metamodel[*]

*an extension to the motivation extension and implementation and migration extension

The capability meta-model is PARTLY based on the work by Bill Poole at JourneyOne.

REFERENCES

(Please note that the links below are good at the time of writing but cannot be guaranteed for the future.)

The following documents havebeen used during the writing of this book:

- ArchiMate 2.1 Specification - www.opengroup.org
- Business gamification for dummies - Duggan, Shoup - ISBN 978-1-118-46693-3
- http://www.knewton.com/gamification-education/
- http://scrummethodology.com/
- Bhushan, Navneet; Kanwal Rai (January 2004). Strategic Decision Making: Applying the Analytic Hierarchy Process. London: Springer -Verlag. ISBN 1-85233-756-7.
- Thomas L. Saaty - AHP - http://www.colorado.edu/geography/leyk/geog_5113/readings/saaty_2008.pdf
- Capability Based Planning with TOGAF and ArchiMate - Bill Poole – JourneyOne

We acknowledge The Open Group for permission to include text and figures derived from its copyrighted TOGAF® Version 9.1 and ArchiMate® 2.1 standards. TOGAF and ArchiMate are registered trademarks of The Open Group

ArchiMate and TOGAF are both registered trademarks of the open group